# Abyssinian Cats

# Abyssinian Cat Owner's Manual

## Abyssinian Cats' Care, Personality, Grooming, Health, Training, Costs and Feeding All Included.

by

Elliott Lang

# Acknowledgements

I wish to convey special thanks to my family members who gave me the time and space I needed to write this book.

I would also like to pay special thanks to my friends and colleagues whose input proved valuable in obtaining all the necessary information I needed to develop this book.

Special thanks to the following organizations/associations for their valuable support:

The American Cat Fanciers Association
America Pet Products Association
Cat Owners Association of Western Australia
The International Cat Association (TICA)
The Governing Council of the Cat Fancy (UK)
Pet Food Manufacturers Association (PFMA) – UK
Sphynx Cat Association
Worldwide Pet Owners Association
The South African Cat Council
The Abyssinian Cat Association (ACA) – UK
Abyssinian Cat Club (ACC) – UK
Abyssinian Cat Club of America (ACCA)
CFA Abyssinian Breed Council

## Table of Contents

Table of Contents

# Table of Contents

Table of Contents

# Table of Contents

# Chapter 1 - Introduction

My love for animals including cats has always been driven by the fact that I have lived with a good number of them right from my childhood. I was brought up in a farm full of different animals and one animal that always fascinated me was the Abyssinian cat, which made me curious to know more about the breed.

Abyssinian cats are some of the friendliest animals you can have at home as pets. It is therefore not surprising that the breed is found in many homes across the world with every established breeder going the extra mile to have the cat as part of his/her breed. From my personal experience, the Abyssinian cat is probably the most people-oriented breed of cat that you can find. The cat however differs from other breed of cats in one unique way: it is simply not a lap cat. Apart from its reputation as a people-oriented pet, the Abyssinian cat is also one breed of cat that is very easy to train. This is due to its inquisitive nature; always out to find out what you do at any given time. The cat is also preferred by homeowners as a pet because it does not only serve as a valuable companion; it also happens to be one of the most loyal pets you can find. Unlike most cat breeds, Abyssinians are lively and attention-seeking cats, which may not be comfortable for some pet lovers. One thing you are most likely to consider when you plan to have an Abyssinian cat is the cost involved. Pricing for Abyssinians can vary a great deal depending on various factors including location, type, breeder and bloodline. However, the general cost of the cat ranges between $350 - £ 208 and $450 - £268 for male and female kittens respectively. An Abyssinian show kitten can cost as high as $1,000 - £595.

Should you be out looking for a lively, active and playful companion, the Abyssinian cat is the best cat to choose. Although its pricing may be on the higher side, its value as a pet is definitely worth its cost.

# Chapter 2 – The Abyssinian Cat

## History/Origin

The origin of the Abyssinian cat remains unclear, although several theories exist as to its exact origin. There are those who believe that the cat is native to Ethiopia, which was often referred to as Abyssinia. There are also those who believe that the cat's origin is in Egypt from where a British solder travelled with a female cat named Zula all the way back to England in 1868.

Due to uncertainty regarding the origin of the cat, geneticists have recently undertaken studies to establish the correct place of origin. The geneticists have since traced the exact origin to the Indian Ocean coastline and along the Southeast Asian coastline.

The conclusions reached by these geneticists have some credence. It is along the Indian Ocean coastline where many indigenous animals from the interior parts of Africa were sold to early merchants to foreigners on voyage. It is therefore possible that the Abyssinian cat was sold along the coast, having been transported from Ethiopia.

It is also possible that the cat is native to the Southeast Asian coastline and, in particular, India. The Leiden Zoological Museum in Holland houses an exhibit of one of the earliest known Abyssinian cat. It is believed to have been purchased between 1834 and 1936 from Calcutta, which used to be a major stopping point for merchants and colonialists.

## The Abyssinian Breed

Although the exact origin of the Abyssinian cat still remains cloudy, available records indicate that development of the breed occurred in Britain. The cat was first exhibited as a breed in 1871 at London's Crystal Palace Cat Show. It was however not until 1896 when the breed was officially registered in the British National Cat Club Stud Book. This paved the way for the formation of the first British Abyssinian Cat Club in 1929. It was also at this time that the breed was introduced in the USA and France. It was not until 1909 that the cat was first exhibited in the USA as a breed.

The first cats exhibited in the USA were not of good quality, which made it necessary for importation of high quality cats from Britain. The arrival of the quality cats in 1930 laid the foundation for the modern USA Abyssinian cat-breeding programs. The breed was then introduced to New Zealand before its introduction in Australia. The breed was actually introduced into Australia in 1959 with importation of two cats from New Zealand and one from Britain. It was not until 1966 when the first Australian Abyssinian cat club; The Abyssinian Cat Club of Australia was formed.

Breakout of the Second World War was a serious threat to the existence of the Abyssinian cat, particularly in Britain. The population of the cat reduced drastically, making it necessary for UK breeders to import the breed from USA to bolster the minimal existing numbers.

The Abyssinian cat is often confused with the Somali cat, a cat that is similar to the Abyssinian except that it has long hair. The Somali cat is believed to be the descendant of the Abyssinian cat, which may also explain the theory that Abyssinian cats are native to Ethiopia. The Somali cat is no longer considered an Abyssinian; it is a distinct breed.

The beginning of the 1960s saw a remarkable increase in the numbers of Abyssinians, mostly in the USA, New Zealand, England and Australia. It is from these countries that the breed spread to other regions of the world. The spread of the breed in Europe was in particular very remarkable, with many homeowners across Europe choosing the cat as their indoor pets.

12

It is also at the beginning of 1960s that many Abyssinian cat clubs and Associations were established in different regions, laying a strong foundation for development of the breed. Many cat breeders indeed abandoned breeding other cat breeds in favor of the Abyssinian breed.

## Myths Associated with Abyssinian Cats

Like with other animals, there are several myths associated with Abyssinian cats. While some of the myths relate to the cat's origin, some are general. Generally, myths are just that, myths. They are not facts that you can rely on.

One myth goes that Abyssinians are the sacred cats associated with Egyptian Pharaohs. This myth has become popular owing to the fact that the cat is similar to cat statues found in Ancient Egypt. While it is a fact that Egyptians held cats in high regard, it is not clear whether the cat has its origin in Egypt. The fact that the Abyssinian resembles those in Egyptian statues does not therefore necessarily mean that the cat originated in Egypt.

The most common myths that are not restricted to Abyssinians but to cats in general is that which states that it is unhealthy to have a cat as an indoor pet. On the contrary, keeping a cat as a pet can be very healthy. Although there are people with allergies, it has scientifically been proven that having a cat indoors as a pet benefits those diagnosed with high blood pressure. This is because blood pressure lowers when one strokes a cat. It is also a fact that people who keep cats as pets are less likely to suffer from stress, as compared to those without cats.

Many people harbor the wrong belief that Abyssinians are not suited as indoor pets owing to the fact they are full of energy and are therefore highly active. While it is true that Abyssinian cats are playful and like to indulge in chasing and climbing, they are territorial and with good training are bound to restrict themselves indoors. In any case, Abyssinian cats are people-oriented and are rarely outdoors alone.

## Pros and Cons of Owning an Abyssinian Cat

### Pros

Abyssinians cats are some of the liveliest cats you can find. You will indeed find them as the best companions you can have. This makes them very suitable to have in homes with the elderly. Abyssinian are also very agile, playful and can be hyperactive or remain quiet, depending on the training that you give.

Because of their highly social nature, Abyssinians are very fond of people they are used to and, in particular, family members. They tend to develop deep affection for family members and will normally show that off in appreciation.

Unlike most cats, Abyssinians do not like to be held in one's lap. They enjoy the freedom of moving around. This makes them very suitable as pets.

Abyssinians are generally receptive to training offered. Coupled with their high intelligence, they tend to avoid dangerous areas and situations as much as possible. Furthermore, Abyssinians are not prone to excessive illnesses and diseases that other cat breeds are prone.

Abyssinians are very cautious animals and uncertain most of the time. This should not hinder you from having one. They are cautious simply because they are the most intelligent cats you can find. An Abyssinian cat also makes a loyal and obedient pet so long as you provide the right training.

## Cons

The hyperactive naturally of Abyssinians makes them unsuitable as pets in homes with very elderly people. Not only are they troublesome for the elderly but they can also feel neglected when attention is not forthcoming.

Abyssinians generally like to climb and will go to great lengths to climb anything in their vicinity. This exposes them to injuries as they can easily fall.

Of all cat breeds, the Abyssinian is probably the breed that seeks attention all the time. They easily get bored and feel lonely when left alone or without any playful engagement.

Because of their playful nature, Abyssinians need a lot of training to behave as expected of them. They can indeed be an embarrassment without appropriate training.

If you plan to have an outdoor cat as a pet then an Aby is not the right pet for you. Abyssinians are generally indoor cats and only venture outdoors once in a while.

One of Abyssinian's biggest disadvantages is the fact that you may be obligated to buy at least two. An Aby only thrives in the presence of another and having one simply makes it feel lonely to an extent that it may not exhibit the unique attractive behaviors that make you want to have one.

Compared to other cat breeds, the Abyssinian breed has few cons. This is one of the main reasons why it is popular across the world. The other reason is its high level of intelligence. It is indeed because of its intelligence that the Abyssinian has been and continues to be crossbred with other cat breeds.

# Chapter 3 - Psychology of the Abyssinian

Psychology of the Abyssinian refers to the breed's mental functions and behavior. As one of the oldest cat breeds, the Abyssinian has been subjected to many scientific studies, studies that have gone to great lengths to understand specific traits that are unique to the breed. It is very important that you acquaint yourself with these traits to help you understand your Aby in order to live with you in the best way possible.

## Understanding Your Abyssinian

The only way you can understand your Abyssinian is to know how it communicates. Like other cats, your Aby communicates through signs and signals. In addition to showing love and affection, your Aby will almost on a daily basis send out signs and signals that you need to interpret. Understanding such signs and signals will go a long way in making your relationship very strong. Your Aby will present such signs and signals in different ways that include:

## Aggression

Although your Aby remains calm most of the time, it is bound to show some aggression in different circumstances. In any case, aggression is a natural feline behavior that can be triggered by different factors including presence of a different pet, a different environment, the presence of a stranger, a hostile environment, when stressed and when being picked up, among other factors. You need to know that there are two types of aggression: offensive and defensive aggression.

You are most likely to observe offensive aggression with a male Aby that has not been neutered. Unlike defensive aggression, offensive aggression is not triggered by anything; your Aby

16

simply becomes aggressive with the intention of intimidating or bullying a fellow Abyssinian, a different pet, or when it wants to be alone. Your Aby will exhibit several signs when in offensive aggression. This includes ears facing forward when walking to a target, constricted pupils, serious focus on target, crouching down in readiness to pounce on a target and a stiff tail before attacking the target.

It is very normal to observe offensive aggression between two Abyssinians, in case you have two or several of them. Like all cats, the dominant male among your cats will want to assert its authority and create clear levels of hierarchy within their territory, something it will accomplish through offensive aggression.

On the other hand, you are most likely to observe defensive aggression in your Aby when it is in danger or threatened. This is a means of self-defense and it will do so with its ears in a flat position facing the tail, wide open eyes, arched back, curved tail, raised fur, open mouth with teeth open, walking sideways toward the enemy and hissing.

There are several causes of aggression in cats depending on the environment and situation. Of all causes, eye contact is probably the main cause. Cats generally perceive direct eye contact as a threat to them and are bound to defend themselves, even when not provoked.

Your Aby will also show signs of aggression when in pain and after a traumatic experience. Something unique about cat aggression is their tendency to re-direct their aggression for something else to you. Your Aby can therefore re-direct its aggression toward a stranger by lurching toward you as a way of letting out the aggression.

There are several ways to deal with your Aby's aggression. Neutering has the positive effect of mellowing your Aby's aggressive tendency. It is highly recommended. Some cat owners whose cats become too aggressive to a point of engaging in regular fights with other cats or pets at home tie a small bell on the collar to warn other cats or pets of the coming of the aggressive cat, giving the others opportunity to move away. The other alternative is to remove what causes aggression in your Aby even if it means restricting it to a specific room or space in the house.

Unlike most cat breeds, the Abyssinian breed is very fond of children and will only show signs of aggression when mishandled. It is therefore very important to educate your kids on how to handle an Aby during play. Like other cat breeds however, your Aby likes to remain in its comfort zone. Your kids can push it to the extreme to a point where it turns aggressive. It becomes necessary therefore to monitor and supervise when kids play with your Aby. It is important to note that your Aby's aggression may not necessarily be a behavioral sign. It can be because of a medical problem, which makes it necessary to consult a veterinarian for assessment.

## Intelligence

Intelligence here refers to your Aby's capacity to solve problems, learn and adapt to its surrounding. From the onset, Abyssinians adapt to new environments very easily so long as they are well treated and provided for. Abyssinian kittens in particular get used to new environments very fast because they set out to explore any new environment to which they are introduced.

Abyssinians also have a very high memory, which contributes to their high level of intelligence. The play activities your Aby engages in do not only serve as its way of life or behavior, it learns a lot from such activities and it is only appropriate that you have many different cat toys. Play activities help them in exercising their minds and in honing their natural skills. However, your Aby's memory will diminish once old-age sets in coupled with occurrence of old age-related diseases and health conditions. Because of its good memory and high level of intelligence, the Abyssinian breed is the easiest cat breed to train. You can literally train your Aby to do almost anything in the house so long as the training does not pose any risk.

## Curiosity

You should not be surprised by your Aby's high level of curiosity. Abyssinians are naturally curious cats that always want to know what happens in their environment. In addition to exploring its room, your Aby will always follow you around, not only for attention but to find out what you do. It will go to the extent of following you outdoors within the compound to explore and to see what is it that you go to fetch.

## Rubbing

Like cats in the wild, your Aby has the natural behavior of marking its territory and everything else within that territory. You will observe your Aby rubbing itself on your legs, on furniture and on the walls. This is a natural behavior that should not be of serious concern. While rubbing itself against anything, your Aby releases pheromones through its scent glands located on its tail and other parts of the body. You have the option of neutering/spaying your Aby in case this behavior is extreme.

## Kneading

Kneading is the behavior of all cats, regardless of breed. You will observe that an Aby, when in a relaxed position on the couch, will push out one of its front paws before pulling it back again. It will do the same with the other paw, sucking clothing in the process. This is a natural behavior that comes first before a cat falls into sleep.

## Body Language

Of all your Aby's signs and signals, the signs and signals it sends out through its body language are very important. Your Aby's body posture at any given time serves as an indication of its state of mind. Your Aby will behave in a particular manner when it is in a relaxed position. Whether lying down or sitting, it will most likely have its legs bent, the tail loosely wrapped and extended. These will be accompanied by normal breathing.

There are times when your Aby will exhibit alert body posture in which case it will lie down on its belly with its back horizontal. Although its breathing may be normal, it will have its legs either bent or extended with the tail curved toward the back. It may twitch its tail from one side to another. This is usually the behavior of a cat focused on something such as live, possible prey.

Tensed cats usually present body posture in such a way that the back remains lower than its upper body while lying down. Your Aby may be moving forward or backwards with its hind legs bent and the front legs extended. The tail may be curled downwards or curled up. This is usually a clear sign of aggression.

Female Abys in particular will once in a while present a body posture where the back of its body is the only part of the body that remains visible with the front part less visible. This can happen when it is lying down on its belly or when in a standing position. The breathing in most cases is usually fast with the tail very close to the body in a curled position. This is usually a sign of anxiety. It can also be a sign that your female Aby is in heat, if it has not been spayed.

You should find it easy to know when your Aby is either terrified or fearful. It will most likely be in a crouched position on its paws with its entire body shaking. The tail will remain close to its body, the tail curled and close to the body. It will probably try to increase its size.

Your Abyssinian cat will not only serve you as a pet and a companion; it will also serve to warn you of possible dangers within the house or compound. Any body language sign or signal your Aby sends out needs immediate attention since it may notice a threat long before you do.

## Vocals

Your Aby will on different occasions meow in different ways that communicate different things. There are times when your Aby will purr, which is usually a sign that it is content. It is however important to note that your Aby can also purr as one way of comforting itself, especially when in pain.

As a companion, the Abyssinian cat is highly responsible. Your Aby will naturally develop the habit of greeting you whenever you come in through the door before rubbing itself against your legs as a show of affection. It will usually do this while meowing in a soft and low tone. This is often coupled with purring.

Loud, high-pitched frantic and repeated meowing is usually a sign of danger or distress. You will need to respond to such calls immediately since your Aby will be in dire need of help.

Your Aby is an attention seeking cat and will do everything it can to have your attention. It will seek your attention through simple meows, which can be loud and high-pitched when your attention is not forthcoming.

## Panting

Although cats generally do not pant like dogs, there are times when your Aby will pant. This will most likely happen while travelling in a car when the cat is stressed and anxious or when the cat is in heat. You must take note of excessive panting, as it may be a sign of illness.

## House Soiling

House soiling is the most disturbing behavior you will most likely observe your Aby engage in. House soiling simply means your Aby urinating or defecating all over instead of the provided litter box.

While it is perfectly normal for your Aby to urinate (spray) outside its litter box, defecating outside the litter box can be because of other reasons. Your Aby will most likely spray outside its litter box as one way of marking its territory. Unlike regular urination, your Aby will spray while standing and probably with one leg raised instead of squatting. Spraying becomes common when you have several cats in the house, in which case the dominant cat (usually a male) asserts its authority.

Urination and defecation outside the litter box can be because of several reasons, one of which is a medical problem. Any inflammation of your Aby's urinary tract will cause frequent and sometimes painful urination. Because it is most likely to associate the pain it experiences with the litter box, it will avoid the same. The other reason may be the urgency to urinate when the litter box is in a different room.

Another reason for house soiling can simply be aversion. Your Aby may find the litter box unsuitable for several reasons including bad odor, a high-sided litter box, a dirty litter box, a distasteful litter box, inappropriate location of the litter box and simple fear of using the litter box.

House soiling can be very traumatizing for you and it is important that you take all measures necessary to find out why your Aby engages in this behavior. It is always recommended that you take your Aby to a vet for assessment when there is no apparent reason for house soiling.

## Confusion

Your Aby may suddenly become confused, in which case it is most likely to get lost in very familiar locations, stare into space, wander aimlessly and forget where its room is located. Confusion in cats is normally accompanied by partial disorientation. Although this is usually a sign of old age setting in, it can also be a sign of illness, which requires vet attention.

## Poor Social Behavior

Abyssinians are generally highly social animals. Your Aby will not be in the habit of avoiding play or greeting you when you come into the house. You may however observe your Aby withdrawing to be alone or simply seek too much attention by becoming over-independent on you. Although this is a sign of old age, it can also be a sign of illness.

# Chapter 4 – Appearance of the Abyssinian Cat

## General Appearance

Although full of energy and therefore very playful, Abyssinian cats can also be quiet and very gentle with extremely soft voices. You can easily identify an Abyssinian cat based on its appearance. The first impression you get when looking at an Abyssinian cat is its wild yet beautiful appearance. You notice how graceful, swift and muscular it is when it walks across the room. It exhibits large almond eyes that stand out on its expressive face.

### *The Head*

The head of Abyssinian cat appears wedged, although with rounded contours. The bridge between its nose and its forehead appears to rise, which gives it the wild appearance. It exhibits large ears that arch forward. Its ears allow it to remain alert all the time. Unlike other breeds of cats that have pointy muzzles, the Abyssinian features a rounded muzzle.

### *The Body*

An Abyssinian cat is of medium size. It features long and slender legs. Its feet are oval in shape and you get the appearance that it is standing on its feet. The cat exhibits a medium long body, looking muscular, full of power yet athletic in appearance, which makes it walk gracefully. The flank is straight and flat with only a slight arch toward the back. This is very pronounced when it is in a sitting position.

## Coat

An Abyssinian features an iridescent coat with short hair. Its coat is very resilient. The coat is soft and fine in texture. It features a unique hair pattern referred to as ticking. This is where you find a single hair with various bands of color.

## Color

You will find Abyssinians in varied colors. Abyssinian cat breeders are very fond of ruddy, tawny, golden-brown, cinnamon, blue, silver and fawn- colored Abyssinians. These are also the colors recognized in championships.

Of all Abyssinian cat colors, the blue Abyssinian cat is one of the most popular. The red Abyssinian cat is the other popular one preferred by some homeowners. The least in popularity is the black Abyssinian cat, and is often ignored by many homeowners.

## Body Weight

Abyssinians are generally light cats. While adult males weight between 8-10 pounds (3-4 kg), females weigh between 6-7 pounds (2-3 kg). Some weigh much more or less depending on diet. Although Abyssinians have a general life expectancy of 12 years, they can live up to 18 years with good care and proper diet.

## Temperament

Abyssinian cat temperament can simply be described as even-tempered. It is the most loving cat you can have at home as a pet. It develops deep affection for its family members and gets along very well with other pets including dogs.

# Chapter 5 - Buying an Abyssinian

There are several ways to buy an Abyssinian, depending on your location and each has its advantages and disadvantages.

## From Your Neighbor or a Friend

This is probably the easiest way to buy an Abyssinian cat. Furthermore, you may not necessarily buy a kitten from a neighbor; you can be given the same as a gift. This way of securing an Abyssinian cat is not recommended. This is because of the risk of acquiring a pet with inherent health problems.

## From a Rescue Center

You are likely to find either a general cat rescue center or a dedicated Abyssinian cat rescue center, depending on your location. While some of these centers offer rescued Abyssinians for adoption, others sell them off to obtain necessary funds for maintaining the pets. Gaining possession of an Abyssinian from an Abyssinian cat recue center may not be appropriate because caretakers are not necessarily knowledgeable about them. This simply means that you will not receive the necessary advice on how to maintain your cat.

## Pet Store

There are dedicated pet stores that offer Abyssinian cats for sale. While some stores are breeder outlets, others are operated by individual owners.

# From a Breeder

The increasing popularity of Abyssinian cat breed across the world has made it possible for establishment of many breeders to cater for increasing demand for the same. Some of the established breeders have a very long history having been in the business ever since the Abyssinian was recognized as a distinct cat breed.

Most established breeders around the world are members of different organizations. Such include The Abyssinian Cat Club of Australasia, The Abyssinian Cat Club of Great Britain, The Abyssinian Cat Association (UK) and The Abyssinian Cat Club of Scotland, Abyssinian Breed Council (UK), Cat Fanciers Association and American Cat Fanciers Association. Some notable breeders include Abayomi (serving Canada and British Columbia), Cedarwood (Canada), Kelela, Bearbrook and Majorus (USA).

Different Abyssinian cat breeder associations from across the world are members of The International Cat Association (TICA), the international organization responsible for maintaining everything relating to Abyssinian cats.

Buying an Abyssinian from an Abyssinian breeder provides several benefits. Although buying from an Abyssinian cat breeder can be expensive, the quality of a cat you buy is no doubt high. This is because breeders put in a lot of effort to ensure that a cat you buy is not only properly vaccinated, but is also free of common Abyssinian cat health problems.

## *How to Choose a Breeder*

Although buying an Abyssinian cat from a breeder is highly recommended, it is very important that you choose an Abyssinian cat breeder carefully. Doing so makes it possible for you to buy a healthy cat.

One of the most important things you need to look into is whether a breeder is a member of a regional or a national association. Such breeders do adhere to code of ethics formulated by associations. A reputable breeder should be available for consultation when it becomes necessary, long after purchasing your cat.

It is also very important that you ascertain whether an Abyssinian cat breeder you plan to buy from has all the requisite certifications and in particular, certifications relating to screening out of genetic health problems.

Perhaps a good way to choose the right breeder is by consulting with your local veterinarian, who is in a better position to know local Abyssinian cat breeders.

## Questions to Ask

There are a number of critical questions that you need to ask a cat Abyssinian breeder before you make any financial commitments. A reputable breeder should not only answer your questions but also welcome such questions. Asking some or all of the questions relating to the following will be of great benefit to you.

## Experience

You need to choose a cat breeder with some years of experience in breeding cats and in particular, Abyssinian cats. It is also important to ascertain whether a breeder participates in cat shows. Breeders who participate in cat shows do not only have the experience but valuable knowledge as well, knowledge that will benefit you, as the breeder will certainly share the same with you.

## Breeding Style

It is very important that you ascertain a breeder's breeding style before you buy. A knowledgeable breeder will normally adopt a breeding style that addresses Abyssinian health problems. Buying from such a breeder ensures that you will buy a cat with minimal health issues to deal with.

## *Vaccinations*

Like with all other animals, it is good to ascertain if a breeder's Abyssinian cats receive the requisite vaccinations before they are sold off. It is very important that you only buy vaccinated cats because they will be your indoor pets.

## *Guarantees*

Although not offered by all Abyssinian cat breeders, buying a cat with health guarantees can be very beneficial to you. A cat that you buy can fall ill within days of the purchase and it is only appropriate that you have some level of guarantee.

## *Certification*

In addition to a breeder's certification, it is good to ascertain whether the parents of a cat you are about to buy are certified. This simply means that a cat whose parents are certified will not be at risk of suffering genetic health conditions.

These are just a few of the many critical questions that you need to ask an Abyssinian cat breeder. Doing so will make it possible for you to buy a quality cat that is easy to maintain in terms of health costs.

## How to Choose a Healthy Abyssinian Cat

The Abyssinian breed is the most popular breed preferred by most breeders. It is also the breed that many breeders specialize in, meaning that most breeders restrict themselves to breeding Abyssinians. One reason for this is the breed's long history and the fact that the Abyssinian cat is people oriented.

Whether buying an adult Abyssinian or kitten, identifying a healthy Abyssinian to buy should not be a problem. One way to go about doing so lies in asking a breeder to see a kitten's parents. The fact that Abyssinians are active cats makes it necessary that you pay attention to its parents' level of activity. A kitten or cat you are planning to buy should also be active.

Your first impression of a cat or kitten you are interested in is also important. Watch out for the cat's behavior towards you. Generally, Abyssinians are receptive and may try out some form of play. Examine the eyes, ears, nose, mouth, anal area, weight and temperament. Ascertain whether a cat you are interested in buying has any discharges from the mentioned areas.

Undertaking a pre-purchase examination is also very important. A reputable Abyssinian cat breeder will normally allow you to visit with a qualified veterinarian for such an examination. A vet should be in a position to perform a number of routine tests including the cat's general blood work, virus tests, stool/urine analysis and general physical examination.

Abyssinian cats are generally expensive, which makes it very necessary that you have a purchase agreement. Reputable breeders do have agreements prepared. Even so, it is important that you pay attention to agreement provisions and in particular sections that address your responsibilities.

## Pure Bred or Crossbred and Why

This is one of the most important decisions you have to make when planning to buy a cat. Like with other cat breeds, you will come across purebred and crossbred Abyssinian cats.

Buying a purebred Abyssinian cat can be beneficial to you considering that you end up with a cat whose personality and characteristics you know perfectly well. Furthermore, buying a purebred cat makes it possible for you to deal with known health challenges that affect the Abyssinian breed. Although crossbred

Abyssinian cats do face similar health challenges as purebred
Abyssinian cats, theirs may be complicated to deal with because
of genetic alterations. The cost of a purebred Abyssinian is
usually higher than that of a crossbred Abyssinian.

## Where to Buy

There are many cat breeders with catteries dedicated to
Abyssinian cats. They include Abyssinian cat UK, Abyssinian cat
NZ and Abyssinian cat breeders UK. This is in addition to other
dedicated breeders in the USA, Canada, France and Australia.

Abyssinian cat prizes vary a great deal. Such factors as breeder,
location, quality of breed and services offered come into play
when determining a cat's prize. The following are just a few of
the many catteries in the USA, UK, Australia and Canada from
where you can buy Abyssinian cats:

### *Osiris (V) Chat d'Or is ([http://www.osirisabyssinians.com](http://www.osirisabyssinians.com))*

This is an established and recognized international Abyssinian cat
breeder. It is a family business owned by Michael Shawn and Sue
Shawn. While Michael bred Abyssinians under the name Osiris in
Brisbane, Sue was busy raising Abyssinians in Victoria, Australia
under the name Chat d'Or. While Michael focused on the
Australian market and has indeed won the "Abyssinian Breeder of
the Year Award" six times since 2009, Sue's focus was both on
the Australian and international market. She established another
cattery in Canada. It is the marriage between the two that
prompted the change of the name to Osiris (V) Chat d'Or Cattery,
after Sue moved her cattery from Victoria to Queensland.

Based in Brisbane in Australia, Osiris (V) d'Or Cattery restricts
itself to breeding Abyssinians. The cattery is registered by
Queensland Feline Association as a breeder. The cattery breeds
quality kittens in terms of health. This is because all their cats
have been tested and certified free from PK Deficiency, a form of
anemia that is a hereditary health conditions common in

Abyssinians. Being a qualified Senior Vet Nurse, Sue has the responsibility of ensuring that all the cattery's kittens are not only socialized but also properly registered and wormed, vaccinated and micro-chipped before they are sold. This breeder is a regular participant in both national and international cat shows organized in different parts of the globe.

### Jodaerin (http://www.jodaerinabyssinians.com)

This is another established Abyssinian cat breeder who started as an Abyssinian cat owner. The cattery name "Jordaerin" is actually the acronym of the family's first cats: Joda and Erin. The name Jordaerin is also the cattery's registered Breeding Prefix. The family was motivated to become breeders after the death of their two cats. They started with other cats donated to them by their friends. The cattery is registered by The Feline Control Council of WA.

Being a small breeder, Jodaerin Cattery only has a limited number of kittens to sell every year. The cattery is a regular participant in cat shows organized across Australia where Jodaerin Abyssinians have always been a favorite of other participants. All the cattery's kittens are not only vaccinated prior to being sold, but are also certified free of PK Deficiency, among other Aby hereditary health conditions.

### Abayomi (http://www.abayomicats.com)

This is a Canadian but international Abyssinian cat breeder based in British Columbia just a few kilometers from Vancouver. Abayomi Cattery focuses on breeding Abyssinians for both the Canadian and USA market. The cattery is registered by both TICA and CFA as a specialized Abyssinian cat breeder.

The name "Abayomi" is an African name common in Egypt and other African countries. It literally translates as "he who brings happiness", the happiness associated with Abyssinians. Abayomi Abyssinians have indeed become very popular not only in Canada but in the USA as well. This is because of the quality, which can be attributed to the fact that the cattery is home-based, meaning that the kittens receive individual attention.

*Abyroad (http://www.abyroad.com)*

This is a small home-based American Abyssinian cat breeder based in one of New York City's suburbs. The cattery is registered by both TICA and CFA. Established in 1984 by Sheila Dentico, the cattery specializes in breeding Abyssinian kittens in both TICA and CFA championship competition colors: ruddy, red, blue and fawn. The cattery's Abyssinian blue kittens are indeed very popular with cat show participants. Being a small breeder, Abyroad only has a few kittens to sell each year, averaging between two and four.

*Crystalpaws (http://www.crystalcats.co.uk)*

Crystalpaws Cattery is an offshoot of the original Crystaltips, which was a cattery that specialized in breeding Siamese cats. The cattery originally owned by Maureen Lear closed down in 1970, paving the way for her son to register Crystalpaws, which is now based in Essex in the UK and specializes in breeding Abyssinians in sorrel, fawn, blue, chocolate and silver colors. The cattery's kittens are regarded as some of the most beautiful in the UK. They are also highly social and free from hereditary health conditions unique to Abyssinians.

*Marafiki (http://www.marafiki.co.uk)*

Marafiki is a family-owned cattery based in Worthing, in South-East England. This is one of the catteries whose owners were first Abyssinia cat owners before turning breeders. The cattery now breeds such other cat breeds as the Ocicat, a breed that is in many ways similar to the Abyssinian.

Marafiki is a Kiswahili language term that literally translates to "friends", something attributable to the Abyssinian breed. The cattery participates in various cat shows where Marafiki Abyssinians have always been admired.

## What Age to Buy and Why

Although you have the option of buying an adult Abyssinian cat or kitten, there are several factors you need to consider before buying. One of these factors has to do with age of your children and in particular children aged below six years. This is in case you have children at home. Although Abyssinians are generally fond of children, having young children at home may make it necessary for you to buy an Abyssinian cat aged two years and above. This will be a cat capable of understanding children.

Being a senior citizen makes it necessary to avoid buying Abyssinian kittens at all costs. This is because kittens can be very mischievous and troublesome. They need constant watching, a task you may not be comfortable performing. You may therefore need to buy an Abyssinian aged at least two years. Note that buying a much older cat may not be appropriate considering that Abyssinians have a general lifespan of 12 years.

How long you plan to spend with your cat is also a very important factor to consider. Buy an Abyssinian aged at least three years in case you will not be at home all the time, unless you plan to have someone at home on a regular basis.

You may consider buying an Abyssinian kitten if you take into consideration the element of training. Abyssinian breeders including Abyssinian cat UK breeders offer kittens aged at least 12 weeks for sale. Although a kitten you buy will have received some level of basic training, you will still have the opportunity to offer the kind of training to suit your home and your preference.

One challenge that you may have when you buy a kitten is in determining its personality. The fact that you are not in a position to determine a kitten's personality at such a young age may make it necessary to buy a mature Abyssinian cat.

## One or More and Why

The decision on whether to buy one, two or more Abyssinian cats depends on several factors one of which is resources. You may opt to buy two cats if you are financially capable of meeting their feeding, care, grooming and health needs. You also need to consider the amount of space you have in your house. Although you may be comfortable only with one, it would be ideal if you buy two for their own company.

## Male or Female and Why

Different people have different preferences when it comes to gender of a pet they plan to buy and Abyssinians are no exception. There are those who prefer buying male Abyssinians and those who stick to buying females.

The most important thing to note is that whether you choose to buy a male or female Abyssinian cat, each gender has its cons. Like with other cat breeds, the Abyssinian male cat will roam in search of mating females. Male Abyssinians also tend to mark their territory indoors and outdoors, which creates an environment where fights may be the order of the day when you introduce another male cat, or a different pet, or in case there is another in your neighborhood.

Like with male Abyssinian cats, a female will also roam in search of a mating partner when in heat. Note that a female Abyssinian, as with other female cat breeds. will come into heat regularly until such a time when they find a mate, a period that can last up to 16 days. Female Abyssinians are usually sexually mature once they attain the age of six months and you may not find it comfortable living with a female Abyssinian in heat, considering that she will keep on calling day and night.

Such problems should not in any way deter you from owning an Abyssinian cat. You can have your kitten or adult cat de-sexed before you bring him/her home. De-sexing is the procedure where cats and other animals are subjected to surgical routines that render them incapable of reproducing. De-sexing literally kills their sex drive. While de-sexing in male animals is professionally known as neutering, it is spaying for female animals.

# Neutering/Spaying

Neutering in male animals including Abyssinian males involves the removal of the testes. This renders your cat sterile, which provides for several benefits. Spaying in female animals, including Abyssinian cats, involves removal of the ovaries and uterus. There are cases where only the ovaries are removed. Like with neutering, spaying also provides for several benefits.

## *Advantages of Neutering/Spaying*

In addition to being a birth control method, neutering/spaying transforms your cat's general behavior. Your male Abyssinian cat that has been neutered will not only show reduced aggressive tendencies; it will also change its mounting and urine spaying behavior. Likewise, your female Abyssinian cat will show less aggression toward males due to reduction in sexual hormone levels.

One of the biggest advantages of having your Abyssinian cat neutered/spayed is the elimination of roaming. Female cats do produce pheromones when they are in heat. Pheromones are chemical signals that attract male cats for mating. A neutered cat does not react on sensing pheromones in the air and will therefore not roam in search for the cat in heat. On the other hand, a spayed female cat is incapable of releasing pheromones and will therefore not roam in search of a male.

The benefits of having your cat de-sexed are not restricted to behavioral changes. There are health benefits as well. Spaying a female Abyssinian cat relieves it of anxiety and stress she would otherwise have when in heat and denied an opportunity to mate. Note that a female in heat can remain in that state for up to 16 days and is bound to be stressed without mating. The female's condition is even made worse by the fact that your cat will come in heat again after about 14 days after the initial phase.

Like with other cat breeds, female Abyssinians are susceptible to mammary cancer, which is mainly caused by reproduction hormones. Spaying reduces the risk of mammary cancer by between 30 and 50%. Spaying also reduces the risk of such health problems as reproduction tract tumors and other associated infections.

Another benefit that de-sexing your cat provides relates to the amount of money you would incur in maintenance. The cost of maintaining a de-sexed cat is very low compared to maintaining a cat that has not been subjected to the procedure.

### *When to Have Your Cat Natured/Spayed*

There is really no fixed age at which you can have your cat neutered or spayed. You only need to consult with your veterinarian to perform the necessary surgical operation. Breeders offer for sale neutered/spayed kittens and cats, saving you the trouble of incurring veterinary expenses. This is a new trend.

Abyssinian cat breeders in the USA in particular neuter male kittens when they are at least four months old. Some breeders neuter them when they are only six weeks old. Likewise, females are spayed when they are of between 5 and 8 years. Some breeders spay them when they only 2 months of age. Contrary to a common belief, neutering/spaying kittens at such a tender age does not hinder their overall development. Neutering/spaying kittens is also beneficial since they have the opportunity to heal faster than when de-sexing is performed when they are mature. Apart from breeders, you can have your cat neutered/spayed by your local veterinarian.

# Chapter 6 – How to Prepare for Your Abyssinian Cat

**What to Know Before You Buy**
There are a number of things you need to know before you buy a pet or an Abyssinian cat for that matter. Knowing some of these things will make living with your cat very easy.

Buying an Abyssinian cat is similar to introducing a new member into your family. You will be obligated to treat your cat in the same way that you do your family members. You therefore need to be prepared to cater for your cat's needs in terms of food, veterinary care, shelter, grooming and love.

Buying a cat is a life-long commitment. You need to be prepared to live with your cat for a long time. Note that although Abyssinians have a general life span of about 12 years, they can actually live much longer depending on their quality of life.

The Abyssinian breed is attention-seeker. You will need to spend a considerable amount of time with your cat. Furthermore, be prepared to be watched keenly. This is because in addition to seeking your attention, your Abyssinian cat will watch everything that you do and do not be surprised if what you thought you had hidden is eventually retrieved.

Although the Abyssinian cat is an in-door pet, it will occasionally want to venture outdoors for activities. Make sure that anything that your cat will climb is safe enough to prevent any unforeseen accidents.

Bring your cat home only when everything is in place. Do not bring the cat home before you have enough food supply and other essentials such as bowls and play toys.

Scratching is an innate characteristic of all cat breeds, Abyssinians included. Ensure that you have a scratch post strategically placed for your cat's convenience.

Although you will occasionally groom your cat, you need to note that it will also indulge in self-grooming once in a while. You will therefore need to make your cat used to a specific spot for grooming.

The biggest thing you cannot ignore when you are about to bring your Abyssinian cat home is cat proofing your house and establishing a safe room. Cat proofing your house simply means making your house as secure as possible for the benefit of your cat. This you can do by removing or storing sharp objects that stand out. A safe room does not necessarily mean a room preserved for the cat. It simply refers to a specific location such as an ideal corner within one of the rooms that your cat will be trained to get used to as its "home".

## Essential Supplies

There is serious need to prepare well long before you bring home your Abyssinian kitten or cat. You will need to invest in a good number of items and equipment for the benefit of your pet. It is very important that you invest in high quality equipment that will serve you for reasonable time. It is not mandatory that you must spend money in buying some of the equipment. Some equipment can be made easily at home if you happen to be a DIY person. The following are some of the most essential items that you must have.

## *Cat Food*

Food is the first item that must have before you bring your kitten or cat home. However, not all cat food will do. You need to buy specially formulated cat food that will allow your cat to grow strong and healthy. It is important to note that cats require specific dietary nutrients and it is only appropriate that you buy food that contains such nutrients.

Specially formulated commercial cat foods are readily available from pet food stores and it is recommended that you check at your local pet store outlet for the same.

You will definitely find cat food in different forms. Dry cat foods contain limited moisture. They are in most cases sprayed with fat to make them palatable. They also contain added nutrition ingredients to replace vital nutrients destroyed during preparation. Wet cat food is usually canned or in foil pouch form. There are also fortified vegetarian cat foods. Because cats are obligate carnivores, their vegetarian food is usually fortified with such ingredients as taurine and arachidonic acid, ingredients that cats are not in a position to synthesize from plants.

It is highly recommended that you buy dry, wet and vegan cat food to allow your cat have a complete diet. It is also highly recommended that you buy cat food from reputable grocers who stock known cat food brands.

## *Food & Water Dishes*

Your cat will definitely eat and it is only appropriate that you buy recommended cat food and water dishes. Just in the same way that you pay attention to color and size of your dishes, you need to choose your cat food and water dishes carefully. Doing so will make it possible for your cat to enjoy eating and drinking.

## Litter Box & Scoops

By natural instinct, your cat will dig and bury its waste. It is therefore very necessary that you buy an appropriate litter box filled with clean litter. You have the option of buying an open or enclosed litter box. Self-cleaning litter boxes have of late hit the market, which you may also consider buying.

## Cat Furniture

Although full of energy and very playful, your Abyssinian cat will occasionally want to rest and catch a nap. Investing in a cat condo is therefore very appropriate. Alongside a condo should be a cat tree. A cat tree is very important because your cat will naturally want to scratch in order to sharpen its claws. Having a cat tree will save you from the agony of having your furniture scratched. An alternative to a cat tree is a cat scratching post in case you have limited space.

## Cat Carrier

It is very important that you invest in a quality cat carrier. It becomes handy when you need to transport your cat to the vet or when traveling. A quality carrier should have enough room where you can have a small cat condo.

## Brush

Investing in a brush is important. This is because your Abyssinian cat will occasionally shed and the brush will come in handy. You will also brush your cat to prevent development of hairballs.

## Collar

This is one of the most important things to have when you bring your Abyssinian cat or kitten home. This is because you never know when your cat will adventure outdoors with the possibility of getting lost. A collar that you buy should have room for your cat's name, your name and address/contact information.

## Non-Essential Supplies

Although generally considered as non-essential cat supplies, some of the following items can be very important, especially when you need to have an active, healthy and intelligent Abyssinian cat as a companion.

Abyssinians cats are generally playful, which may make it necessary for you to invest in cat toys. Alternatively, consider using such readily available items like paper bags and cardboard boxes when playing with your cat.

Although your cat will naturally scratch as one way of sharpening/cutting its claws, you may need to consider investing in a cat nail clipper for trimming its claws.

Feeding your cat dry, wet and vegetarian food should be enough to cleanse its teeth. You may consider buying a cat toothbrush and paste just to ensure that you cleanse its teeth well.

## Licensing

Bringing an Abyssinian cat home as a pet is similar to enlarging your family. The breed indeed develops closeness and unique attachment to all family members and considers itself part of your family. This is one of the reasons why you need to license your Abyssinian cat. Licensing your cat is similar to buying insurance coverage. Licensing it makes it easy for animal control officers to reach you should your cat become lost.

The other reason why you need to license your cat relates to disease control. You give out vital information to animal control officers when you license your cat. Data captured during licensing benefits you in a great way. This is so because you will be contacted in case of newly available vaccinations. More importantly, licensing your cat makes it easy for animal officers, cat breeders and animal health authorities to have vital statistics necessary for planning.

Different countries have different legislations that relate to pets, including cats. There are countries where cat owners are not obligated to buy licenses for their cats but must buy them for dogs. There are also countries where licensing is compulsory for all pets.

Cat licensing requirements and fees differ across the Unites States of America. While it is mandatory in such cities as Los Angeles for dogs to be licensed, licensing is not required for cats. Likewise, there are states where it is mandatory for cats to be licensed. In addition to licensing, cat must carry proper identification. In such states, licensing is by a county's relevant animal authority. There are also states where veterinarians are given the responsibility to license cats. This is so because cat licenses are meant to last for the duration of vaccination. Cat owners therefore find it easy to renew their cat licenses when returning their cats for vaccination.

Cat licensing is mandatory in the UK. In addition, your cat will need to have a cat tag. Cat licensing in the UK is the responsibility of different authorities concerned with welfare of cats and other pets. However, most licenses are issued by local authorities at the local level. Cat owners can also buy licenses or renew their licenses at animal care centers.

It is important that you do not view licensing your cat as a legal requirement. View it as one of the most effective ways of protecting your cat. You also need to consider registering your Abyssinian cat with your local Abyssinian cat club or association if you happen to live in an area with an established cat club. This applies in cases where you live in a jurisdiction where licensing of cats is not mandatory.

## Micro-Chipping

Micro chipping refers to the latest technology use in identifying lost animals and pets. Unlike externally attached Radio Frequency Identification tags commonly used to identify farm animals, micro chipping involves implantation of a small Radio Frequency Identification chip just under a pet's skin.

You can have your Abyssinian cat micro-chipped. This is a service offered by veterinarians. You will have the chip implanted under your cat's skin at the back of its neck. This is the area where there are layers of connective tissue capable of holding the chip in place. Although use of microchips is not yet widespread, there are jurisdictions where you are obligated to have your cat or other pet micro-chipped.

There are several benefits that you derive from having your cat micro-chipped. From the onset, it becomes easy for animal control officers and animal shelter organizations to contact you if the cat becomes lost. Having your cat micro-chipped is also beneficial to you considering the fact that cat or pet registries, veterinarians and trainers use microchips to identify pets under their care.

Because of the importance of micro-chipping many breeders, including Abyssinian cat breeders UK, microchip their stock before selling them. The chip contains all the information that you provide, including your name, residence and contact information.

## Introducing Your Cat to Your Home

Just in the same way that you take time to get used to a new environment, your Abyssinian cat will take some time to get used to your home. Your cat may not behave in a way you expect during the first few days. It will certainly not eat and behave as you expect.

Like with any cat breed, the Abyssinian breed is a territorial animal. This is why it is very important that you designate for it a room or space in your house. Your cat will naturally spend the first few days or weeks learning every sound and smell in its territory before venturing into other rooms. One of the most important things that your cat will learn is your body language and the tone of your voice. It is therefore very important that you take all these into account when communicating with your cat.

Your main task during the first few days should be to introduce your cat to its important tools. This is the time to introduce it to its litter box, feeding dishes, water dishes and furniture. Abyssinians are generally fast learners and will follow minor instructions to the letter. This is also the right time to introduce one or two toys for play.

Introducing toys will make your cat get involved in play activities, which will go a long way in eliminating boredom. You will need to spend the first few days observing your cat with the aim of ascertaining its demands, which you will need to fulfill. The main point here is to make your cat feel as comfortable as possible. One thing you are most likely to observe is its act of hissing and growling at any new sound or movement. This is normal and should not be a concern.

## Introducing Your Cat to other Pets

Bringing your cat home when you already have other pets can be a serious challenge. This is because the resident cat already considers your home its territory and will not welcome another cat very easily. To prevent such a scenario, it is always recommended that a cat you introduce should be of the opposite sex of the resident cat. Note that you will not be able to prevent catfights even when both of them are de-sexed.

The easiest way to introduce your Abyssinian cat to another is to set them apart. You need to create a separate room or space for your new cat and let them bond naturally. Bringing in a new cat and housing them in the same room or space can be very problematic.

## Introducing Your Cat to Family Members

Introducing your cat to family members and in particular to children the first time you bring it home is not recommended. Doing so can be stressful to the cat. It can actually feel very uncomfortable and take very long to get used to its new environment.

Introducing your cat to family members depends on how fast it gets used to its room or space. While some cats take between two and four weeks to get accustomed and start interacting with family members, others take as little as few days.

It is recommended that you do not introduce your cat to several family members at the same time. Only one family member should venture into the cat's room or space with the aim of bonding with the cat. For easy bonding, a family member venturing into the cat's room or space should not stand but rather sit on the floor when communicating with the cat. A light touch is recommended for the cat to get used to the family member and build trust.

Abyssinians are generally inquisitive and will naturally walk slowly toward a family member they are not used to. It is therefore very important that a family member who ventures into the cat's room or space for the first time keeps his/her distance and let the cat walk towards him/her.

One rule of thumb that any new family member venturing into a cat's room or space for the first time should not do is to pick up the cat. Abyssinians are not lap cats and do not like to be carried around. Family members also need to note that there are times when the cat will want to have its peace and will show this by hiding underneath its furniture or bed. It should simply be left alone when this happens.

46

There are several ways by which you can introduce your Abyssinian cat to other family members quickly. The first of these is for a family member venturing into the cat's room or space to engage the cat in play activities with use of toys. Bringing the cat small amounts of food is also another great way for your cat to bond with other family members.

It can be a serious challenge to bring an Abyssinian cat to a home with a dog as another pet. It is always a good idea to keep your cat indoors in its room or space before you allow it to venture into other rooms or outdoors. Even so, it will be beneficial to keep the dog on a leash to allow the cat explore its new surroundings. You will need to give your cat room to approach the dog on its own terms. Because your cat will naturally approach the dog to sniff it, you will need to be prepared to act when necessary, just in case the dog is not welcoming.

The first few days or weeks upon bringing your cat home will be a very involving and challenging one. It is therefore very important that you create enough time to be at home most of the time to ensure that your cat remains comfortable as much as possible. The challenge eventually wears off once the cat gets used to the home, family members and your other pets.

## Mistakes to Avoid

There are several serious mistakes that most new cat owners and, in particular Abyssinian cat owners, do that you need to avoid at all costs. Avoiding these mistakes goes a long way in helping your cat get used to its new environment fast enough.

One of the serious mistakes you need to avoid is failure to make your home pet-friendly. You need to make your home pet-friendly by ensuring that all that your cat will need is in place before you bring it home. Create for your cat a special room or space. You also need to equip the room or space with all that the cat will need. These include litter box, cat furniture and food/water dishes among other vital equipment.

Abyssinians are people-oriented cats and one of the costly mistakes you need to avoid is to leave your cat alone for a lengthy period. Leaving your cat alone for a long time can easily drive it into developing a feeling of loneliness, increased anxiety and undesired behaviors. Make it a point to have someone at home most of the time, as your cat will need companionship.

Abyssinians are clever and highly intelligent cats. They are very receptive to training, which you need to embark on as early as possible. Although certain training aspects will definitely require a professional trainer, teaching your Abyssinian cat obedience commands should not be a problem. Ensure that your cat can positively respond to such minor commands as sit, stay and leave. A cat that follows commands will rarely develop untoward behavior.

Every home has rules that family members are obligated to stick to and your home is no exception. As part of your family, do not fail to make your cat aware of simple rules particularly when it comes to feeding time. It cannot only be embarrassing but injurious for your cat to pounce on your hands when you are presenting its food. You need to avoid such behavior by getting your cat used to sitting before feeding. This is something that the rest of your family members must be aware.

Another serious mistake you need to avoid is to give your cat too many treats. While treats are an effective way of rewarding your cat whenever it does something positive such as following instructions, giving too many treats negates the value of training. You need to use dispense treats sparingly. Restrict dispensing of treats to those occasions when your cat does something extra.

One of the costly mistakes that new Abyssinian cat owners make is neglecting to socialize with their pets as much as possible. Like with dogs, failure to socialize with your cat makes it fearful and it can easily develop aggressive behaviors. It is therefore appropriate to introduce your cat not only to family members but to your visitors as well.

Abyssinian cats are generally indoor pets. However, they need to exercise as much as possible to remain healthy. One of the mistakes you need avoid is to restrict your cat indoors. It is always good to take your cat out for walks, giving it an opportunity to climb trees, which is its nature. Doing so allows your cat to release pent-up energy that it would otherwise channel into undesirable behaviors.

A common mistake that most cat owners commit that you also need to avoid is failure to keep your cat mentally active. Many cat owners limit themselves to socializing with their cats, forgetting that keeping their cats mentally active is also beneficial. Like with other pets, cats kept without mental activity become easily bored. Engage in play activities using cat toys. Hide such toys and let your cat find them.

Abyssinian cats are very adorable, which makes many Abyssinian cat owners commit one serious mistake: failure to punish their cats when they engage in untoward behavior. Because physical punishment is likely to instill fear in your cat, consider using a harsh tone when communicating and expressing your disapproval for a behavior that does not impress you. These are just a few of the mistakes you need to avoid if you need to have a well-behaved and obedient Abyssinian cat as a pet. Failure on your part will simply mean having a pet that you cannot control, which will be a recipe for serious problems at home.

# Chapter 7 – Care for Your Abyssinian Cat

## Basic Care

Like with all cats, your Abyssinian cat will depend on you for everything including basic care. Although your cat will to some extent be independent, you will be obligated to provide it with suitable and healthy food, shelter, veterinary care training and love. It is only with appropriate basic care that you will be able to develop strong a rewarding relationship with your cat.

Apart from such necessities as food and shelter, proper hygiene is mandatory as part of basic care. Your cat needs to be in a clean environment at all times. Do ensure that all equipment, including litter box, food/water dishes, playing toys and the room, remains clean all the time. Cats are generally clean pets and do not be surprised when your cat avoids the litter box, feeding and its room. That will be a clear sign of an unclean environment.

Basic care also involves your cat's safety. You need to know where your cat is every time you are at home. Although Abyssinians are generally indoor pets, they occasionally venture outside to enjoy the sunshine and explore the home environment. This is where cat collars and ID tags become useful just in case your cat wonders off and gets lost.

Just in the same way that you and your family members visit your physician for regular check-ups, your cat also needs to visit a vet for regular check-ups. You do not need to wait for your cat to show signs of illness to take it to a vet. It is during such check-ups that minor signs of illness can be diagnosed and proper treatment administered. This is one of the most important basic care routines that you cannot ignore in order to have a healthy cat as a pet.

Closely related to regular check-ups is feeding. Failure to feed your cat nutritious food can easily lead to medical problems. You need to avoid the practice of feeding your cat dog food. Cat nutritional requirements differ in a big way with dog nutritional needs and feeding your cat dog food simply denies your cat vital nutritional supplies.

Grooming is a very important part of your cat's basic care. You will still need to groom your Abyssinian cat even though it has short hair. Doing so will be very effective in reducing development of hairballs and matting. In addition to grooming, you will also need to clip your cat's claws.

Training your cat is a very important part of basic care. By their nature, cats generally know how to do their own things, which, regrettably, may not be proper. Beginning training early goes a long way to preventing such habits as jumping on the kitchen counter, scratching the couch and eating plants. Note that it is through training that your cat comes to learn about applicable house rules.

Although cats generally know how to entertain themselves, Abyssinian cats in particular can be very playful. It is therefore very important that you regularly engage your Abyssinian cat in play activities using cat toys and other suitable items. Engaging your cat in play activities provides for valuable benefits including strengthening your relationship. Furthermore, playing with your cat on a regular basis provides it with the physical strength and mental stimulation it needs.

There is nothing more valuable than giving your cat proper basic care from the moment you bring it home. Giving your cat basic care can indeed be beneficial to you since you will prevent common cat diseases that can otherwise be costly when you have to take your cat to a vet for treatment. It is also by giving your cat proper basic care that you get to have a well-behaved cat at home as a pet.

## Living Quarters

Your cat's living quarters is its most valuable location. Although your Abyssinian cat will obviously venture into other rooms and in particular the living room, there are times when it will naturally retreat to its living quarters. This is usually the time when it needs to catch a nap or simply relax. This makes it very important to know how to treat the living quarters.

Whether you have enough room at home and have designated a room to your Abyssinian cat, or just created a special place in one of the rooms as your cat's living quarters, the room or space needs to be as clean as possible. You need to maintain cleanliness in the room or space as much as possible to make your cat feel comfortable. That cleanliness extends to ensuring that the litter box(s) and everything else in the room or space remains clean.

Just in the same way that you arrange your rooms in the best way possible, you need to ensure that your cat's living quarters are properly arranged. Do ensure that the litter box is far away from feeding/water dishes. The scratching post should also be strategically located for your cat to find it easy to perform its scratching ritual.

## Grooming

"The only self-cleaning thing in this house is the cat". This is a very common phrase used on many refrigerator magnets and for good reason. By their nature, cats are the epitome of cleanliness. They will go to great lengths to ensure that they remain clean at all times. This is why you will notice your Abyssinian cat "licking" its face and other parts of the body with the tongue.

The licking is not actual licking. It is actually a means through which your cat cleans itself, using the tongue as a washcloth. Cats generally have unique tongue. The tongue is barbed, making it useful for a good number of purposes. It uses its tongue as a grooming tool, using it to remove loose fur, stripping away the scent of food, getting rid of such parasites as fleas, increasing blood circulation and to control its body temperature. In grooming itself, your cat will naturally apply saliva on its forepaw before embarking on the grooming routine.

The onset of self-grooming starts right when a cat is born. The mother naturally "licks" its kitten to not only keep them clean but to arouse them to suckle, to stimulate them to remove body waste (feces and urine) and to provide them with comfort, especially when it is hot. For the kittens, self-grooming starts when they are about four weeks old.

It is very important to know how your cat grooms itself to enable you know how you will groom it. When self-grooming, your cat will apply saliva to the inside part of one paw before cleaning itself in an upward circular pattern. It will naturally start by cleaning its nose before proceeding to the eyes, backside of the ears and eventually the forehead. Your cat will do the same with the right paw. It is only after this that your cat will embark on grooming such other parts of the body as its front legs, shoulders, flanks, genital area, hind legs and the tail. This can be a time-consuming exercise, which can last for an hour.

The importance that cats in general attach to self-grooming makes it very necessary that you too come in to groom your cat. Indeed, Abyssinian cats, just like other breed of cats do enjoy grooming. Grooming your cat does not only make it clean, doing so also goes a long in developing a strong bond between you and your cat, in addition to allowing you to screen for any skin problems.

There are several ways to groom your cat and one of these is brushing. Although Abyssinians do not have long fur, frequent brushing prevents the development of hairballs, which in extreme cases require surgery to remove. Brushing your Abyssinian cat once every week should be enough. You need to invest in a quality de-shedding tool whose use requires gentle strokes to prevent pain. You also need to have a soft grooming brush to use alongside a de-shedding tool.

Remove mats from your cat's body. Although Abyssinians generally are not prone to mats due to their short fur, it is good to keep your cat on the safe side by removing mats that you notice. Mats can be extremely painful to a point where your cat will not be able to move. Although frequent brushing reduces the risk of mats, you need to invest in quality clippers just in case.

Ensuring that your cat's ears and eyes are clean through grooming is very important. You need to examine your cat's eyes and ears for any signs of debris that you need to clean out to prevent buildup of the same. The ears are in particular prone to build up of wax that you need to remove frequently. You need to invest in cotton swabs and cotton balls that are effective in cleaning both the eyes and ears. You however need to be careful when cleaning your cat's ears. Restrict yourself to cleaning visible areas only.

Although your cat will naturally indulge in its natural habit of scratching at the scratching post, you still need to examine its nails to ensure that they remain as short as possible. Make it a habit to trim your cat's nails only once in a month using a quality clipper. One area you need to avoid reaching when clipping is the triangular area of the claw that is usually pink in color. Referred to as the quick, cutting into this area leads to bleeding, which can make it very difficult to clip your cat's nails next time since it will naturally develop fear. It is important to note that you only need to clip the front paws. The hind paws rarely grown long.

Unlike dogs, cats rarely need bathing. It is however important that you bath your Abyssinian cat at least once a week. It is also during bathing that you can effectively use your cat brush to smoothen and straighten its fur. You need to invest in quality medicated soap, shampoo and conditioning for bathing.

**Grooming Products**

There are a good number of cat grooming tools in the market that you need to invest in to make your cat clean, healthy and comfortable. These include brushes, flea/tick combs, sprays, shampoos, conditioners, clippers, scissors and lint-removal tools. Some of the notable brands include Andis, Bio-Groom, Evercare and Oyster among other brands.

Although ignored by some cat owners, taking time to groom your Abyssinian cat is very important. You need to set apart at least an hour once a week to groom your cat. This is because Abyssinians have short fur and generally enjoy grooming.

## Transportation

Cats and Abyssinian cats in particular make valuable pets. Not only are they adorable and make good companions; they cheer you up when you are down, in addition to making you remain active as you engage them in play. It is however regrettable that you may not move with your Abyssinian cat(s) as you may wish to do. This is because unlike dogs that like and enjoy traveling in a car, cats do not. Traveling with your cat in the car makes it very uncomfortable. Cats can vomit, urinate and become dehydrated while traveling.

You need to invest in a quality cat carrier in order to transport your cat without any problems. A carrier you buy should be spacious enough to allow your cat to stand, turn around and stretch. It should also be very comfortable. The best way to transport your cat using a carrier is to have your cat get used to it several days before you travel.

As part of transport preparation, it is recommended that you consult with your vet for appropriate transport advice, particularly if you plan to travel with your cat over a long distance. Your vet will be able to prescribe medications and sprays that will calm your cat during the journey, in effect eliminating stress that affects cats when being transported.
Food usually plays a major role in the comfort of a cat when traveling in a car. Your cat will most likely vomit if you feed it just minutes before you embark on travel. It is recommended that you feed your cat at least two hours before you set off to prevent vomiting. One serious mistake you need to avoid when traveling with your cat in the car is to let it out when you stop along the way. Your cat will become confused and possibly run away. You can only let it out if you have a leash.

## Exercises

Abyssinians are generally indoor cats even though they occasionally venture outside just to explore the exterior part of the house. Although advantageous, their being indoors most of the time presents a challenge. Depending on the type of food, how frequently you feed your Abyssinian cat and the kind of treats you give it, your cat can easily gain excess body weight, which is a foundation for serious health conditions.

The only effective way to help your cat in maintaining a healthy body weight is through exercise. Exercising your cat is also beneficial even if it does not gain excess body weight. Exercising your cat goes a long way to ensuring that it remains physically fit.

By their nature, Abyssinians and cats in general are highly flexible animals and can perform different types of exercise. One of the simple exercises you may consider giving your cat is the use of laser pointer. Moving the laser around at different heights will give your cat a good opportunity to stretch as it moves to paw the light on a wall.

You definitely cannot ignore the importance of cat tree when it comes to exercising your cat. Having a cat tree gives your cat a good opportunity to exercise as it climbs it. The other benefit of having a cat tree lies in the fact that you do not need to be around for your cat to exercise; it can do so even in your absence. In absence of a cat tree, you need to ensure that there are no obstructions to windows so that your cat can jump on the windows as it pleases.

Having plenty of cat toys is beneficial to your cat in terms of exercise. Because of their playful nature, you need to have different types of cat toys that allow for different types of exercises. You may alternatively use readily available items from home instead of buying toys.

Many cat owners have of late found their treadmill valuable in exercising their cats and you too may consider the same if you happen to have one at home. Although your cat will learn quickly how to walk and run on the mill, you will need to supervise it very closely.

One form of exercise you cannot ignore is taking your cat out for walks occasionally. A simple walk along the road or in a park exposes your cat to a new environment, which in itself provides other benefits.

## Cat Toys

Ensuring that your Aby exercises on a regular basis is very important and there is no better way than to do so than with cat toys. Cat toys provide for opportunity to exercise both body and mind. Not only does your Aby's body remain physically fit; its mental health is also enhanced, in the process relieving stress in addition to improving blood circulation within the body. Cat toys are also very effective in training a cat to abandon retrogressive behaviors while at the same time acquiring progressive behaviors.

There are basically four types of cat toys that you need to invest in:

## Wand Toys

A wand toy does not need to be a special item. You can make use of a stick or a piece of cloth. Twitching (stick) or waving (cloth) in circles will look very enticing to your Aby. This is because such an item's movement becomes similar to a potential prey. You can add other enticing items on the wand that makes it attractive and encourages your Aby to keep on playing. Such other items you can add on the wand include colored feathers.

It is very important that keep the wand away from the cat once play session is over. Your Aby should not get used to the wand because that may negate its usefulness during play. It will be similar to a cat getting used to a prey to a point that it does nothing when the prey passes by. There are different wand brands in the market if you choose to buy.

## Ball Toys

Balls are very effective as cat toys. Unlike ordinary balls however, cat ball toys are small. To your Aby, the movement of these balls on the floor resembles scampering of potential prey, which entices your Aby to a point that it chases after the balls. Like with a wand toy, a good way to effectively make use of cat balls is to add some niceties on the balls, niceties that your Aby will strive to chase and grab. You have the option of buying Ping-Pong balls, sponge balls or Mylar balls among others.

## *Food-Dispensing Toys*

These are the best toys to have when you plan to leave your cat at home for a long time in any given day. These toys literally deliver the food to your Aby whenever it engages in play with them. One great benefit of these toys is that they teach your Aby to work for its food, with the work being the play activity. This engages its mind, teaching it new tricks in the process. You can indeed make use of cat treats with these toys. Like with the other toys, there are different brands of ball food-dispensing toys in the market.

## *Catnip Toys*

Catnip is a stimulating herb that cats really enjoy eating. Catnip toys are designed in such a way that they allow you to stuff catnip in them. The amount of catnip you stuff in is very critical because your Aby can be over-stimulated.

Regardless of which cat toys you decide to buy, the toys should be those that bring out your Aby's natural instincts. The toys should mimic prey to encourage your Aby to not only engage in play more but also master requisite techniques or behaviors.

## Caring for a Pregnant Abyssinian Cat

Although you have the option of buying a spayed Abyssinian kitten/cat, you may also choose to buy one not subjected to the procedure, in which case it is bound to become pregnant when a partner is available or when you take it to a vet for that specific purpose. Caring for a pregnant Abyssinian cat, just like with caring for any pregnant cat, differs greatly from caring for a non-pregnant cat in many respects.

From the onset, you need to know whether your cat has become pregnant. This should be at the earliest possible time so that you adjust a number of things to suit its condition. Generally, a cat's gestation period ranges between 60 and 70 weeks and although you are not able to ascertain whether your cat is pregnant through urine or blood tests, there are specific signs for which you need to watch out.

The first sign of a cat's pregnancy is what is usually referred to as pinking up. This is the enlargement of a cat's nipples in which case the nipples not only become enlarged but become pink in color as well. You are able to notice this when your cat is about three weeks pregnant.

Like in human females, pregnant cats gain weight naturally when pregnant. You will notice a gradual increase in weight when you hold your cat and notice the pregnancy if you are observant. Increase in body weight usually occurs at the same time when pinking up occurs.

Another simple and clear sign of cat pregnancy that can help you know whether your cat is pregnant is morning sickness, just in the same way it happens to human females when they become pregnant. Clear signs of morning sickness in cats manifest in excessive sleep, especially during morning hours and failure to eat or avoid certain foods.

It is important that you take your cat to a vet for confirmation of pregnancy. A vet will professionally ascertain your cat's pregnancy through palpitation. Even so, this will only be possible when the pregnancy is around four weeks. A vet may also opt to do an ultrasound in ascertaining pregnancy.

With your cat's pregnancy confirmed, you need to quickly adjust several things. Your vet should indeed be in a position to inform you which adjustments you need to make, one of which is nutrition. Your pregnant cat will need increased amount of nutritious food. Amount of food should however not be excessive. This will prevent labor problems when the time comes for her to give birth.

This is also the time to ensure that your cat has access to safe drinking water at all times. You also need to allow your cat have as much rest as possible. She should only be engaged in play when she initiates the same. Your cat requires close monitoring during the whole period of pregnancy. Your vet will most likely advise you on when to take your cat for check-ups.

Apart from nutritious food, water and visits to the vet for check-ups, you need to buy equipment and supplies in readiness for your cat giving birth. These include kitten box, surgical gloves, syringe/eyedropper to aspirate nose/mouth secretions, cotton thread for ties, scissors, clean towels, antiseptic for cleaning umbilical and kitten milk replacer.

The last week of your cat's pregnancy is a very critical moment. Introduce her to the kitten box, which you need to place in a quiet, warm location away from children. Because your cat is likely to spend much time in her new location, you need to make food and water readily available.

There are a number of things you will notice when your cat goes into labor. Fist, her mammary glands will have increased tremendously in size. She will also most likely start nesting and have a general change of behavior.

Although you have made every effort to provide your cat with a kitten box, it can occur that your cat may choose to give birth elsewhere within the house. This is perfectly normal and should not be a cause of concern. You will only need to transfer her and the kittens to the kitten box.

It is natural that your cat will give birth without your help. You however need to watch her very closely. There are several scenarios that require you to call the vet since they are emergency situations. These include excessive high body temperature, unpleasant smell of discharge, contractions lasting more than 20 minutes without any signs of kitten and protrusion of placenta through the vulva without any sign of a kitten.

Taking care of the kitten should not be a big problem since your cat will do almost everything. You will however have specific responsibilities toward your cat. In addition to ensuring that you maintain a high level of hygiene in your cat's room or space, you will need to ensure that your cat receives a nutritious diet and supplements that properly feed the kitten. The kitten will be able to start feeding on solid food when they are between four and five weeks, with introduction of solid food being on gradual basis.

It is only after six weeks that you can start weaning the kitten to ready them for sale, or to give them as gifts. Abyssinians are very social animals and it is very necessary to socialize the kitten as much as possible. The period between eight and ten weeks of their lives is particularly important. This is the time the kittens need to be socialized, which can be by exposing them to your family members and letting them explore other spaces and rooms in the house.

One of the most important things you cannot ignore once your cat gives birth is the need to have the kittens wormed and vaccinated. Your vet should be in a good position to advise you on when this should be done.

It is important to point out that although your cat can take up to between eight and ten weeks to become pregnant again, the possibility that she can attain another pregnancy at two weeks after giving birth is usually high. This is one of the reasons why many cat owners choose to have their female cats spayed. You will therefore need to take precautions to prevent your cat becoming pregnant again soon after giving birth, unless you intend it to be so.

One serious challenge you may face once your cat gives birth is if your cat rejects her kittens. This can be very challenging since you will have the responsibility to hand raise the kittens. Generally, Abyssinians give birth to few kittens, in most cases between three and four kittens. It should however not surprise you to find out that your kitten has given birth to up to six kittens.

# Chapter 8 – Feeding

## Nutrition

Your cat requires appropriate nutrients necessary for body development, growth and general function of the body. These nutrients reside in the food that you feed your cat. Failure to feed your cat nutritious food definitely leads to specific nutrient-deficiency illnesses/diseases, some that are obviously life threatening. Just in the same way that you pay close attention to what you eat, you also need to pay attention to what you feed your cat. Pay attention to the labels on cat food, which inform you of the nutritional value of the food.

Of all nutrients, water is probably the most important nutrient that your cat needs, although it cannot survive on water alone. The fact that a big percentage of your cat's body weight is literally made up of water makes it very necessary that you supply your cat with fresh drinking water on a daily basis. Lack of water in the body does not only interfere with smooth metabolism; it can also be a cause of serious illnesses.

Your cat also needs sufficient amounts of protein. Proteins play a very important role in the body and in particular in the formation of body cells, tissues, enzymes, organs, antibodies, enzymes and hormones. Your cat's body also requires proteins for the repair of body tissues and proper maintenance of the body.

Closely related to proteins are amino acids that your cat also requires. Amino acids are literally the building blocks of proteins and while your cat's body can easily synthesize non-essential amino acids from its diet, its body cannot naturally synthesize such essential amino acid as taurine, which makes it necessary for your cat's food to contain the same.

Your cat does not only require water and proteins. It also requires fats. Fats are very important when it comes to production of specific hormones and in cell structure. Fats are also required by the body for proper utilization of certain vitamins. The food you feed your cat must contain such essential fats as linoleic and arachidonic acids. Lack of these fats can easily lead to your cat suffering from reduced growth and skin problems.

As has already been indicated elsewhere, Abyssinians are playful and therefore require a lot of energy to remain active. This is why you need to feed your Abyssinian cat carbohydrates. Carbohydrates do not only provide your cat's body with the energy it requires; carbohydrates play a critical role in maintaining good health of the intestines. You however need to note that cats are generally carnivorous animals and therefore need little carbohydrates.

Vitamins are the other very important nutrients that your cat needs. Different vitamins play different roles in the body with some vitamins required for enzyme reaction. Since your cat's body cannot synthesize most vitamins, it is very necessary that the food you feed your cat contain all the required vitamins. Like with the other nutrients, lack of vitamins leads to occurrence of various vitamin-deficiency illnesses.

Lastly, your cat requires sufficient supply of minerals for proper bone and teeth development, for metabolic processes and for maintenance of appropriate fluid balance within the body. Because your cat's body cannot synthesize minerals, you must ensure that your cat food contains these vital inorganic compounds.

Although your cat definitely needs different nutrients to grow and remain healthy, the amount of nutrients you feed your cat is very critical. This is because cats require different amounts of nutrients depending on their age.

## Kitten Nutrition Needs

You definitely have no role to play when it comes to feeding kittens nutrients. Kittens obtain all the nutrients they need for their first few weeks from their mother's milk, which contains all the necessary nutrients. There are instances where the kitten's mother is not around because of death, illness or when the mother rejects her kitten upon giving birth. In such instances, formulated commercial milk is always the best option.

Kittens generally grow very fast during the first few weeks of being born. The commercial milk you buy must therefore contain adequate amounts of all the nutrients in balanced quantities. It is important to point out that kittens do require energy three times that of adult cats and proteins two times that of adults.

## Adult Cat Nutrition Needs

Meeting nutritional needs of an adult cat can be a serious challenge. Not only should an adult cat have enough to eat but also consume a diet rich in all the necessary nutrients. An adult Abyssinian cat is not only active and therefore requires increased amount of energy; it also requires increased amount of proteins for repair of body tissues and other body functions. It also requires increased amount of essential fats particularly during cold weather. Although it is very necessary that you feed your cat on these, you need to be careful so as not to make your cat obese.

It is very important to note that although your adult cat will need the same amount of nutrients during adulthood, there are exceptions. During the times your cat is sick or pregnant; you may need to adjust the nutrients your cat consumes.

## Old Cat Nutrition Needs

Just in the same way that feeding kittens and adult cats differ, feeding an older cat also differs. You are most likely to start noticing your Abyssinian cat's aging signs when it is about twelve years. Because of the body composition, metabolic and immunologic changes it is bound to go through, occurrence of such age-related diseases/health conditions such as loss of muscle mass, arthritis, obesity and dental problems among others become common.

Taking into account the changes in an old cat's body and the likelihood of development of the indicated diseases/health conditions, a diet for an old cat should be one that promotes good health and appropriate body weight. Such a diet should ideally be low on carbohydrates but high on proteins, vitamins, essential fatty acids and minerals.

## The Right Food

You have two options when it comes to the right food for your cat: canned and dry food, which at times is referred to as dry kibble. Compared with canned food, dry food has low water content, high carbohydrates and is high on plant proteins. Considering that cats are carnivorous animals, dry kibble is not the right food for your cat.

Although your cat needs food rich in protein, it is better off with animal-based protein. Feeding your cat plant-based protein derived from vegetables simply has no value to your cat in terms of nutrition. Unlike plant-based protein, animal-based protein contains amino acids, the essential fats that are beneficial to your cat. Canned food contains animal-based protein, making canned food the right food for your cat.

Although canned food cannot be said to be that fresh, dry kibble goes through a lot of processing in addition to being cooked at high temperatures for long times. This not only lowers the quality of protein within, but also damages other nutrients.

The importance of canned cat food over dry kibble is also in the amount of water contained. Cats generally do not drink water since their prey in the wild supplies them with enough water. Having a cat at home therefore requires that you feed it on a diet rich in water, which makes canned food the right food for your cat.

You have two options when it comes to cat food. The first option is to prepare cat food on your own at home or buy commercial canned foods. It is important to look at these two options to enable you to make the right decision when it comes to food for your cat.

Unknown to some cat owners, cats are carnivorous animals and therefore rely on eating raw meat. Whether it is fresh or raw meat is unimportant since wild cats kill their prey and may not consume the whole prey in one instance. Cat owners who do not feed raw meat to their cats deny them what they are actually supposed to eat. A common belief by such cat owners usually has to do with the element of food poisoning.

Unlike us humans, who are highly susceptible to food poisoning, cats are not. This is because while the food we eat resides in our intestines for anything between 35 and 55 hour, the food that a cat eats only resides in its intestines between 12 and 16 hours. This simply means that any harmful bacteria remain within a cat's intestine for a short period, unlike in humans. This short period lowers the risk of food poisoning.

It is therefore perfectly appropriate to buy raw meat to feed to your cat. Even as you do so, you need to remember that not all raw meat sources are the same in quality. You need to consider buying whole cuts of meat that you can thoroughly clean before feeding your cat, instead of buying pre-ground meats available in supermarkets.

It can be very fulfilling if you opt to prepare for your cat its food at home. Even as you do so, it is very important that you do subject your cat to the same meat source. You seriously need to consider changing meat sources. You have the option of feeding your cat on beef, rabbit meat or chicken among others. You also need to consider adding in some water and recommended supplements.

The second option is to go for commercial cat food, specifically canned cat foods. There is a serious challenge you are about to face when shopping for canned cat food: marketing gimmicks or food labels. Some of the food labels you are most likely to come across on canned cat foods include "For Indoor-Only Cat", "Natural", "Premium", "Breed Specific", "Veterinarian Recommended" and "Therapeutic Diet" among other labels.

Although they seem very promising, some of the food labels can be very misleading. The reality is that most canned foods with these labels contain wheat, corn, soy and by-products. While wheat, corn and soy definitely have high levels of carbohydrate that your cat does not really need, the by-products happen to be the only source of protein for your cat, which is not appropriate.

The only effective way to overcome the challenge presented by promising yet false food labels is to look at both the composition and ingredients used in making canned cat food when shopping. While the composition part of it refers to the percentage of fat, protein and carbohydrates that the food contains, ingredients refer to the specific nutrients in the food. You need to pay attention to three important things when it comes to choosing the right canned cat food. It should be food that is high in water content, low in carbohydrates and contain animal-based protein instead of plant-based protein.

It is worth pointing out that mainstream canned cat foods can at times be very expensive, depending on your location. This is because they do contain the muscle meat of chicken and turkeys, among others. This is normally listed as the first ingredient. Depending on your financial position, you may consider buying canned cat foods that contain by-products. These are normally labeled as "chicken by-products" or "turkey by-products" among others. The fact that they are affordable does not mean that they are of no nutritional value.

Like with all canned foods, canned cat foods do feature preservatives and ascertaining the kind of preservative used in cat food is very important. There are canned cat foods that contain such preservatives as ethoxyguin, BHA and BHT. These chemicals have been proven unsafe when used as preservatives. Although most cat food manufacturers have abandoned the use of such preservatives, you need to check to ensure that the canned cat food you are about to buy does not contain the same.

## Feeding Program

There is no uniform cat-feeding program. This is the frequency at which you need to feed your cat. How you frequently feed your Abyssinian kitten, adult cat or an old cat definitely differs. This is because they need to feed at different intervals and in different amounts at every stage of their life. Your home environment and type of food you feed your cat also informs feeding frequency.

Just like with human babies, kittens need to be fed small amounts of food at regular intervals. This is because their tummies are not yet capable of handling large amounts of food. This is the time they need sufficient amount of various nutrients necessary for growth and development. Kittens generally need to be fed at least four meals spread out in any given day.

Unlike kittens that need to eat nutritious food for growth and development, your adult Abyssinian cat needs to eat maintenance food. Maintenance food aids in further development of the body

70

and helps maintain strong healthy bones, as well as enhances the body's immune system. Because it can be difficult to ascertain the amount of food that your adult cat needs, it is better to let it eat until it is satisfied. Two meals in any given day should be enough.

Old cats are generally susceptible to various diseases and health conditions that make it necessary to tailor your cat's feeding frequency, taking into account any health problems it may have. The same goes for sick kittens and adult cats.

It is important to look at the feeding program for adult cats because such is the cat you are most likely to have. You have two options when it comes to designing a feeding program for your cat. Your first option is to let your cat become accustomed to a free feeding program, where you fill its feeding dish with large amount of food that it can eat when it wishes. Although this program best suits a cat that is often left alone at home for a considerable amount of time, it has its disadvantages. First, you will be obligated to buy kibble cat food because fresh food may not last long in the open. Secondly, there is the risk of your cat over-eating and therefore becoming obese.

Your other option is to design a scheduled feeding program where your cat gets used to a specific time when it is served food. This program can be very beneficial considering that you are literally in a position to control how much food your cat consumes at any given time.

The fact that you have designed a feeding program for your cat should not mean that such a program is permanent. There is always room to alter the program depending on different situations. Such variations might include traveling, when your cat is sick, when your cat is pregnant (if a female and not spayed) and when adverse weather changes occur.

## Food Allergies

Like people, cats too develop different allergies including inhalant, fleabite and food allergies. In the case of food, cats generally develop food allergies when subjected to specific food on a regular basis. Abyssinians do develop allergies when they are between two and six years although a few have been noted to develop food allergies as early as five months old. They can also develop these allergies as old as twelve years of age.

Contrary to a popular belief, a food allergy does not necessarily mean food intolerance. Unlike food intolerance that manifests itself in the form of diarrhea or vomiting, food allergies exhibit real symptoms that may include itchy skin, hair loss and excessive scratching.

Causes of food allergy in cats are usually specific ingredients found in cat foods and in particular in such cat food as corn, soy, dairy products, wheat and seafood. It is worth noting that these are the same foods found in dry or kibble cat foods.

Determining whether your cat suffers from food allergies can be a very big challenge. This is because food allergy symptoms are in most cases similar to those presented by such cat diseases/health conditions as fleabite allergy and intestinal parasite hypersensitivity. There are several ways by which you can determine whether your cat suffers from food allergies or other diseases, although determination can take some time.

The most effective ways through which you can determine whether your cat suffers from food allergy is to undertake a food trial. This means subjecting your cat to a specific type of food for several days while looking out for any allergy symptoms. It is important to note that blood tests are only effective in diagnosing other types of allergies, but not food allergy.

There are instances where your cat's food allergy and associated symptoms become serious. This is usually the time to take your cat to a vet for treatment. Your vet will most likely feed your cat fatty acids, steroids and prescribe antihistamines as the first line of treatment. The only effective way of treating food allergy in cats is avoidance of causative food.

## What Not to Feed Your Abyssinian Cat

Food that is edible to you and/or your dog may not be edible to your cat. Feeding your cat certain foods cannot only cause allergies and intoxication, consumption of certain foods can easily lead to your cat going into coma and possibly death.

It is perfectly normal to have alcoholic beverages at home so long as you keep them safe and away from your cat. Your cat will definitely become intoxicated when it consumes any food containing alcohol and can easily go into coma with high chances of dying.

Spices make food very tasty but only for humans. Feeding your cat spices can cause serious allergic reaction and toxicity, which can lead to death.

Cats are carnivorous animals and therefore do well with meat but not bones. Whether from fish, beef, lamb or poultry, bones are simply dangerous to your cat. Not only can they cause obstruction, bones can also lacerate your cat's digestive system and cause serious problems.

You should not feed or let your cat eat such foods as tea, chocolate, coffee and caffeine. These contain caffeine, theophylline and theobromine. These ingredients cause vomiting and other health problems in cats.

While both human vitamin and mineral supplements can indeed be healthy, they can be very dangerous when you feed them to your cat. You need to keep all your food supplements far from reach of your cat.

These are just a few foods that you should not feed your cat. Although your cat will naturally avoid some of these foods, you need to keep away those that it can accidentally consume.

## Cat Treats

Giving your cat treats occasionally is highly recommended. Contrary to common belief by some cat owners, cat treats are not entirely valueless. Modern cat treats are formulated to encourage good dental, digestive, general, hairball and skin health, depending on the type of treat you buy. Note that there are crunchy, dental, soft, jerky and catnip/grass cat treats. You also have the option of buying grain-free, natural or organic cat treats. To enhance their appeal and taste, cat treats are in most cases flavored. You may choose to buy beef, chicken, vegetarian, turkey, and tuna or fish flavored treats.

Your cat definitely needs an intake of calories, which cat treats provide. However, it is very important that you measure the amount of treats you feed your cat. Because cat treats largely contain calories, they should not make up more than 10% of your cat's calorie intake. Your cat should obtain the remaining 90% from quality nutritious foods.

Like with shopping for canned cat food, it is important that you choose cat treats with utmost care. This is because some information contained in the labels may not be correct. You seriously need to look out for the amount of calories a cat treat food contains before you buy.

When to feed your cat treats is very important. This is because there is increased possibility of your cat developing addiction or taste for treats instead of its regular foods. Because of this, you need to feed your cat treats only on special occasions. These can be rewards for doing something positive like mastering a rule or excelling in an exercise.

Because cat treats basically contain calories, they are not recommended for overweight cats. Feeding your overweight cat treats will simply worsen its condition and increase the risk of serious health conditions. For an overweight cat, go for catnip/grass treats. Both are cereal grasses and therefore low on calories.

You should be able to find different types of cat treats in the market. There are those that are soft and moist and those that are hard, similar to dry cat food. You cat will most likely hate dry treats in favor of soft treats. It is always a good idea to balance between the two for your cat to receive all the nutrients it needs for good health.

There is a number of cat treat brands on the market and just like with choosing canned food carefully, you need to choose cat treats carefully. The most important things to look into are the ingredients a treat contains. This is very necessary because some cat treats may contain ingredients that may cause allergies.

How you store cat treats you buy is of great importance. The Abyssinian is a very clever cat and will notice when you feed it treats. It will therefore look for the same wherever you store its canned food. It may develop the habit of stealing treats if you fail to store them in a secure location. The best way to go about storing cat treats is to store them in a different location from where you store its regular food.

# Chapter 9 – Training

## Cat Training

Cat training refers to the practice of instilling certain values in your cat. It is a wide area that involves changing some of your cat's natural but unpleasant behavior. Cat training provides for several benefits not only to you but to your cat as well. A well-trained cat usually has its body and mind well-stimulated, which goes a long way in enhancing its overall health. Well-trained cats also exhibit good behavior, especially in the presence of visitors. It is also through training that you build a close relationship with your cat. Failure to train your cat properly can easily turn your cat into a pest instead of a pet.

Cat training requires that you first understand your cat in different respects. Luckily, Abyssinians are not only highly intelligent but also very easy to train. You can easily train your Abyssinian cat to stop doing something or to behave in a certain manner at certain times. Like other animals, cats do learn through experience. Your Abyssinian cat will stop doing something you dislike with a little training.

You have two options when it comes to training your cat. You have the option of taking your cat to a dedicated cat or pet training center, invite a cat or pet trainer to your home or undertake the training on your own. Because taking your cat somewhere else or engaging the service of a trainer involves expenses, you may consider undertaking the training on your own. Training your cat personally can be very fulfilling, especially when you see your cat positively responding to your instructions.

One thing you must avoid at all costs when training your cat is punishment. Unlike dogs, cats respond negatively to reprimands and punishments. Punishing or reprimanding your cat for failing to follow given instruction develops fear in your cat, which makes training very difficult. Furthermore, a fearful cat will always try to run away. The secret to training your cat effectively lies in using treats. Rewarding your cat with treats whenever it does something positive or when it responds positively and follows given instructions is the only sure way to give your cat proper training. There are three basic areas where you need to train your cat: house training, behavioral training and trick training.

## House Training

You share almost every room in your home with your Abyssinian cat. Although it will tend to spend most of its time in its room or space, it will occasionally venture into the other rooms for companionship or to simply explore the other rooms. This makes it necessary to train it properly in different areas.

Litter training is the most important house training that you must give your cat. You must ensure that the litter box is not only clean at all times, but also placed in the most appropriate location within the cat's room or space. One reason why cats avoid the litter box and choose to urinate in other places in the house is usually due to dirty litter. Note that what may seem clean to you may not necessarily be clean to a cat. You need to get accustomed to changing the litter on a daily basis before you can embark on litter training.

You need to start introducing your cat to its litter box immediately after you bring it home. Although filling the litter box with dry and clean soil will naturally attract the cat when it needs to use the bathroom, you still need to introduce your cat to it. It is highly recommended that you place the litter box away from the cat's sleeping quarters. Apart from litter box training, you need to train your cat where to sit or lie when in the living room.

77

## Behavioral Training

Cat behavioral training is probably the most extensive and difficult part of cat training. This is because of the many behavioral changes that you need to train your cat to adopt or discard.

Your cat naturally has hunting instincts and will naturally bite or claw your hands when you engage it in play activities. Although this is a perfectly normal cat behavior, you can train your Abyssinian cat to abandon this behavior. The best way to offer the training is during play sessions where you stop play immediately when it bites or claws. This is also the best time to use treats, denying your cat the treats when it engages in biting and clawing.

Your action of stopping the play and denying it treats sends a strong message to the cat. You are mostly likely to notice changes in your cat's behavior in play sessions that follow, as it learns that it is not acceptable to claw and bit. This is also the time to effectively make use of treats, rewarding it for not biting and clawing.

Cats do communicate by meowing. You cat will naturally meow when hungry, when in danger, when in need of a mate (like a non-spayed female cat), to attract your attention or when requesting something. Although perfectly normal, excessive meowing can be a serious problem in the house. Your first reaction to your cat's excessive meowing should be to consult your vet with the aim of ascertaining whether your cat suffers from illness or disease. It is also important to note that such changes in the house, like re-arranging furniture, can make a cat meow a lot. It is equally important to note that you may be the cause of excessive meowing if you have made your cat develop the habit of meowing by giving it something whenever it meows. The most effective way to train your cat to stop excessive meows is to give something like a treat when it is quiet and denying it the treat when it meows.

While having a playful Abyssinian cat as a pet is perfectly in order, it can be a big challenge when you have a hyperactive and playful Abyssinian cat. Your hyperactive cat will indulge in such activities as too much play, hiding things in the house, chasing unseen mice, jumping on and off furniture and in extreme cases, stealing.

Cats that do exhibit these behaviors are in most cases hyperactive cats that are not engaged in play activities and often left alone. The most effective way to get your cat to abandon these behaviors is to provide means such as play activities through which your cat can expend the excess energy. In case of an un-spayed or un-castrated cat, this may also be the right time to have it castrated/spayed.

One of the most misunderstood cat behaviors by many cat owners is a cat's territorial behavior. Like such other wild cats as Leopards, your Abyssinian cat will naturally mark its territory within the house, which can be every room and items in the house including furniture. Note that cats have a keen sense of smell and will detect any foreign smell, however light that may be.

Your cat has scent glands located along its tail, on its front paws, either side of its forehead, on its chin and its lips. Its behavior of rubbing its tail or head on you or anything else in the house is therefore not a way of grooming itself but a way of marking its territory. The cat can smell each place it has marked.

Although it is naturally normal for your cat to mark its territory, this marking can be extreme. Note that cats engage in this behavior as one way of guarding themselves from possible threats. The scent they leave behind when marking is meant to serve as a warning to other cats that the area is already occupied. The only effective way to train your cat to abandon this behavior, that at times can be irritating, is to socialize with your cat as much as possible. Your cat should never feel threatened in any way.

Having an untrained cat at home as a pet can be very dangerous in a case where you also have a bird or birds as pets. By their nature, cats have hunting and chasing instincts. Although your cat may not chase after prey to kill for food, it will chase out of instinct with the aim of tossing the bird around, which can result in serious injuries to the bird. This is predatory behavior that is very common with indoor cats like Abyssinians.

Persistent predatory behavior stems from the fact that your cat will not have opportunity to vent out its natural instincts and therefore directs the same to the potential in-house pet. The only effective way to offer predatory training is to have your cat socialize with a potential prey under close watch. Such socialization makes the cat realize that the potential prey is indeed part of the family.

## Nocturnal Training

Your Abyssinian cat is naturally a nocturnal animal. It will spend a lot of time sleeping during the day and become active during the night when you are deep asleep. Its night activities can be very disturbing if you do not offer appropriate training. Your cat will naturally become active from late in the evening to early morning.

Letting your cat get used to this schedule will deny you quality sleep. The most appropriate training you offer should aim at changing its schedule of activities, which you can do by engaging it in play activities during the day instead of letting it sleep. Because changing its schedule can be challenging, you need to go about doing so gradually until it gets used to the new schedule.

Even so, you will not completely stop your cat from engaging in night activities. You therefore still need to make available suitable cat play toys to allow your cat engage in some activities during the night. You will however need to set up the toys away from your bedroom to avoid disruption of sleep.

## Trick Training

One reason why Abyssinians make good companions is the fact that they are receptive to trick training. You can train your Abyssinian cat to do a number of things in the house including ringing the doorbell or playing dead.

## Dominance Training

Although your Aby is naturally independent and can easily defend itself against attacks by other cats, there are times when dominance training becomes necessary. It is through dominance training that your Aby gains the confidence it needs when in the presence of other cats. This training is particularly useful in cases where you live in an area with many other cats in the neighborhood and your Aby ventures out a lot.

## Command Training

This is one of the most important trainings you can give to your Aby. Your Aby should be able to positively respond to such commands as come, roll, go and sit. This training requires a lot of time and patience on your part because your Aby will obviously not master all the commands immediately.

## Leash Training

Walking on a leash is the other important training you must offer your Aby. This is so because you will occasionally take your Aby out for walks. Because cats are generally not receptive to leashes, you need to expose it to the leash long before you embark on leash training. It is highly recommended that you place the leash near its food dish or other favorite location, where it sees it often and gets used to it. It pays to buy a harness specially designed for cats. These leashes have the leash attachment located behind the harness and not at the neck.

## Training Rules

- Regardless of the type of training, be patient but committed to the training schedule.
- Never resort to punishing your Aby in case it fails to perform as expected. Punishing it will make it develop fear and therefore fail to master any training that you offer.
- It pays to embark on training at a slow pace, training a single skill for several days before introducing another item.
- Always reward your Aby whenever it performs better, for encouragement.
- Set a specific training time every day. This will get your Aby accustomed to the training routine.

# Chapter 10 – Health

## Abyssinian Health

One reason why cat lovers prefer Abyssinians to other breeds is because the Abyssinian breed stands out as one of the healthiest breeds to have. It is also because of their good health that most Abyssinians live past their average lifespan of about 12 years. With appropriate diet, regular veterinary check-ups and vaccinations, your Abyssinian cat can live to attain the age of 15 years.

## Common Illnesses/Diseases

Although generally healthy, your Abyssinian cat is still susceptible to specific diseases/conditions unique to the breed. Most of the illnesses/diseases are hereditary.

### *Gingivitis*

Gingivitis is a periodontal disease. It causes inflammation of the gums that turn reddish. Plaque formation also occurs. Plaque is basically a collection of debris, food, dead skin, mucous and bacteria. The gingival surface however remains very smooth. The disease can easily be reversed at the earliest stage through proper dental care.

Without proper dental care, the disease develops further with development of calculus under the gums. Calculus is a mixture of organic matter, carbonate and calcium phosphate. In addition to further development of plaque, the gum surface becomes irregular with some pain in the gums.

As the disease progresses, it forms a narrow space between the teeth and the inner wall of the gum. The bacteria present in this space mutate and release toxins that damage gingival tissue. Occurrence of gingivitis is common not only in cats but also in dogs aged three years and above.

Apart from the swelling and reddishness of the gums, other symptoms of the disease include bad breath. Gingivitis is largely caused by accumulation of plaque. There are also other risk factors that encourage occurrence of the disease. These include excessive soft food, old age, bad chewing habits, diabetes, breathing through the mouth, crowded teeth and autoimmune disease among other risk factors.

Because of the danger that gingivitis poses to your cat, you need to help your cat in preventing occurrences of the disease. This you can do by ensuring that your cat's oral health remains at its optimum by brushing its teeth at least twice in a week with veterinarian toothpaste, or using a finger pad to clean the teeth. This simple action will go a long way in preventing build-up of plaque.

A serious case of gingivitis requires veterinarian attention at the earliest possible time. In addition to a physical examination, your vet will as a matter of routine try to establish possible causes of the disease, which can be the kind of food you feed your cat.

There are several ways your vet may choose to treat the disease, depending on his/her findings. Your vet may prescribe antibacterial solution for squirting on your cat's teeth to prevent build-up of plaque, prescribe dietary supplements or prescribe specific foods that help in promoting good dental health.

In case of serious gingivitis, your vet may choose to remove baby (deciduous) teeth that may cause teeth overcrowding, which is a cause of the disease, or remove the affected teeth. It is also possible that your vet may choose to only remove plaque and calculus before polishing the surface of your cat's teeth.

Gingivitis is a serious gum disease that you must not let your cat suffer from. This is so because it reaches a stage where your cat will not be able to chew food properly, or even eat, due to pain. You will certainly not rule out malnourishment and possible death of your pet.

## *Familial Amyloidosis*

This is not a disease but rather a health condition that affects the liver. It is actually a group of disorders with similar characteristics: abnormal deposition of amyloid (a fibrous protein) into body tissues. Amyloid occurs as a hard and waxy substance and develops from the degeneration of tissue. The disposition interferes with the normal functioning of areas where the protein has reached. Familial Amyloidosis is a hereditary health disorder common in Abyssinian, Burmese and Siamese breed of cats.

Although this is a hereditary disorder, it can also be caused by various factors including chronic infection, inflammation of inner layer of the heart caused by bacterial endocarditis and tumors. The condition presents several symptoms including general body weakness, loss of appetite, excessive thirst and urination, vomiting, enlarged abdomen and swelling of the limbs accompanied by joint pain.

Familial Amyloidosis is not treatable. It is a disorder that impairs the liver, seriously affecting its function and that of other body organs. Most cats die from the disease. There are specific measures that your vet can take to lessen the pain and help prolong a cat's life. Your vet may take such measures as blood transfusion, fluid therapy, diet changes and in some cases, surgery.

### *Retinal Atrophy*

Retinal atrophy is a non-treatable hereditary disease common in some cat breeds including the Abyssinian. The disease is also common in some dog breeds. It is the degeneration of the retina, causing gradual loss of vision, which ends in blindness. The disease presents such symptoms as decreased vision at night, dilated pupils and cataract formation among other symptoms.

### *Hyperthyroidism*

This is an endocrine disorder whose occurrence is directly linked to over-activity of the thyroid gland, which leads to excess levels of specific hormones. These hormones play a very important role in the body, the role of controlling metabolism. Increased levels of these hormones have the negative effect of increasing your cat's heart rate with the possibility of your cat developing a heart murmur. Left untreated, the disease can easily cause heart failure, kidney damage, high blood pressure and death.

Your cat will exhibit a number of symptoms when infected. These include diarrhea, vomiting, behavioral changes, weight loss, increased thirst and urination, body weakness, poor condition of the coat and rapid heartbeat among other symptoms. These symptoms may not necessarily point at hyperthyroidism because other cat diseases, including cat diabetes and renal failure, present the same symptoms. It is therefore very important that you take your cat to the vet once you notice any of these symptoms.

The fact that hyperthyroidism does not affect a specific breed of cats means that all cats are at risk of suffering from the disease. It mostly occurs in older cats (and dogs). There are two main ways of treating hyperthyroidism. A treatment method a vet chooses depends on your cat's medical condition.

Your vet may choose to prescribe such medications as Tapazole whose action is not to treat but to control the disease. Your cat will need to use prescribed medication for the rest of its life. There are instances when a vet may choose to undertake surgery with the aim of removing an enlarged thyroid. The other treatment your vet may choose to implement is radioactive iodine treatment, which involves injection of a single dose of radioactive iodine. Iodine has the positive effect of destroying the damaged part of the thyroid while leaving normal thyroid tissues intact.

## *Pyruvate Kinase Deficiency*

Pyruvate Kinase is an enzyme whose deficiency in your cat's body leads to impairment of red blood cells, greatly reducing the ability of red blood cells to metabolize. The inability of red blood cells to metabolize causes anemia in addition to other blood issues. Pyruvate Kinase deficiency is very common in such breeds of cats as the Somali, Abyssinian and other short-haired cat breeds.

Caused by defects in genes acquired at birth, Pyruvate Kinase deficiency presents such symptoms as body weakness, anemia, jaundice and increased heart rate among other symptoms. This condition is usually addressed through bone marrow transplant, which is the only treatment method available. In addition to being an expensive treatment, it is also life threatening. Most cats that suffer from this condition die by the time they attain four years.

The indicated diseases/health conditions are just a few of the health problems to which your Abyssinian cat is susceptible. There are however other cat diseases/health conditions that your cat may acquire depending on your environment, your cat's diet, living conditions and whether there are other cat breeds in the house or not. Some of these include:

## *Arthritis*

Arthritis refers to negative changes that occur within joints. These changes develop when cartilage that protects different bone joints wear out, causing friction at the joints. The friction causes swelling accompanied by pain. Although the cartilage is supposed to be replaced naturally, arthritis is bound to occur when it wears out faster than it is replaced.

Just like in humans, onset of arthritis in cats is in advanced age, although middle-aged cats can also suffer from the condition. The swelling and accompanying pain is usually chronic, which causes a lot of discomfort.

Arthritis does not have a cure. It can only be treated with any treatment that a vet offers aimed at lessening the pain and swelling that your cat experiences. Treatment needs to be offered at the earliest possible time to prevent further loss of cartilage.

Although arthritis is common in such other cat breeds as the Himalayan, Siamese and Persian cat breeds, your Abyssinian cat can suffer from the condition due to such factors as old age, obesity, congenital defects, accidents and infection.

Arthritis has a serious effect on your cat's health. This is because it does not only make your cat uncomfortable but impairs its mobility as well. The condition presents such symptoms as limited activity, stiffness in walking, limping and social withdrawal.

Although your vet will definitely prescribe medications that help in preventing swelling and managing pain, he/she is likely to recommend the most appropriate diet for your cat as the most effective treatment option. This is because food plays a very important role in your cat's overall health.

### *Allergic Dermatitis*

Allergic dermatitis refers to conditions that affect the skin negatively. These can be caused by such factors as food allergy, parasites, hormonal imbalances and infections. One effective way to avoid allergic dermatitis in your cat is to feed it on food rich in meat-based protein, essential fatty acids and antioxidants.

There are instances when you may need to take your cat to a vet. This is when the skin is not only rough but has wounds. Your cat's skin should be smooth and soft without any signs of flakes. Hair on the skin should also be evenly spread out.

## Diabetes

Just like in humans, cats suffer from diabetes when their metabolic system cannot effectively control the amount of sugar in their blood. The main cause of this is usually lack of or limited production of insulin, which is produced in the pancreas. Apart from insufficient amount of insulin, your cat is at risk to become diabetic when it is obese, approaching old age, is a male, stress, poor diet and hormonal imbalances.

Diabetes presents several symptoms including excessive thirst, rapid weight loss, loss of appetite, vomiting, increased urination and general body weakness among other symptoms.

Once diagnosed, your vet may recommend a number of ways to help your cat cope. One of the most effective solutions your vet is most likely to recommend is diet and the kind of food you feed your cat. A vegetarian diet with proper nutrient profile is usually very effective in managing diabetes in cats.

## Gastrointestinal Disorders

These disorders also include disorders of the cat's digestive system. These disorders hinder smooth digestion and absorption of nutrients contained in the food that your cat eats. Gastrointestinal disorders in particular interfere with both the intestine and stomach, causing pain and in some cases swelling. Some of these disorders include acute gastroenteritis, colitis, diarrhea, constipation, irritable bowel syndrome and pancreatitis among others.

Occurrence of these disorders does present several symptoms including vomiting, flatulence, body weakness, constipation, diarrhea and in some cases regurgitation.

Although they do not present any immediate danger, gastrointestinal and digestive disorders can become life threatening if not addressed in good time. You need to take your cat to a vet for correct diagnosis and treatment. Treatment options available aim at alleviating the pain and suffering that your cat experiences in addition to eliminating symptoms. One of the most effective treatment options available relates to the food that you feed your cat. Vets recommend highly digestible foods for cats with these conditions. Other recommended food types include high soluble foods.

You will be obligated to prevent occurrence of these disorders for the benefit of your cat. This will mean ascertaining specific factors or foods that may be the cause of such disorders.

### *Heart Disease*

Your Abyssinian cat is at risk of suffering from heart disease, and like with most cat diseases, the food you feed your cat plays a major role in preventing or encouraging the disease. There are other factors that may cause heart disease in your cat. These include old age and heartworm, among others.

Heart disease has the negative effect of enlarging your cat's heart, making it inefficient. In effect, the heart holds more fluid than it is supposed to hold. A clever way to go about preventing excessive fluid in your cat's heart is to feed it cat food low on sodium.

Heart disease presents several symptoms, some similar to those presented by other cat diseases. These include low-pitched cough, difficulty in breathing, weight gain/loss and abdominal swelling among other symptoms.

## Kidney Disease

Kidney disease is one disease that is often ignored when looking at cat diseases. All cats regardless of breed are susceptible to kidney disease. The kidney plays an important role in a cat's body by removing waste from the bloodstream and regulation of fluids in the body. Failure by the kidneys to play these vital roles puts a cat's life in serious danger.

Kidney disease presents different symptoms including loss of appetite, frequent vomiting, depression, poor coat appearance and frequent or no urination. Kidney disease can be acute, sudden and chronic or long-term. It can be caused by such factors as trauma, surgery, shock, serious blood loss, poison, drugs, infection of the kidneys and obstruction of urine.

Unlike other cat diseases that present symptoms almost immediately, symptoms associated with kidney disease only appear when a large part of the kidneys are already destroyed. It is therefore very necessary that you take your cat for regular veterinary checkups.

## Urinary Tract Infections

UTIs are various infections that affect both the bladder and urethra of cats. Of the infections, feline idiopathic cystitis (FIC) is the most prevalent. Thought to be caused by excessive levels of stress, it causes inflammation of the urinary tract in addition to formation of crystals along a cat's urinary tract. Such crystals are in most cases those of calcium oxalate.

UTIs present different symptoms including inappropriate urination, straining during urination, loss of bladder control, colored urine, licking of the genitals, loss of appetite and lack of interest in any activity among other symptoms.

UTIs can be caused by several factors including obesity, diet composed of foods rich in magnesium, calcium, phosphorous and protein 9unbalanced, surgery and infections. Any UTI can be very problematic since occurrence rate remains high after treatment. This becomes real when causative factors are not addressed before treatment is offered. Vets emphasize the need to feed your cat on the right cat food that is not only nutritious but also well balanced.

## *Obesity*

Acquisition of food in the wild for any creature including the Abyssinian is not an easy task. Cats in the wild have to literally hunt and chase their prey. The physical exertion definitely takes a toll on their bodies and it therefore is not easy to find an obese cat in the wild. Things are different for domesticated cats, including Abyssinians. Domesticated cats have it very easy when it comes to food simply because all that they eat is readily provided, which poses the risk of obesity.

According to a research study conducted by the Association for Pet Obesity Prevention (APOP) in 2011, over 50% of cats were found to be either obese or overweight. It therefore simply means that your Aby, being an indoor pet, is at risk of becoming obese even though it is one of the most active cat breeds.

Simply put, your Aby is most likely to become obese when its energy intake is more that the amount of energy it requires. Just like in humans, its body converts the extra energy it consumes into fat, which are then deposited in specific locations within its body. Getting rid of deposited fat can be a big challenge even with regulation of energy intake.

Living with an obese Abyssinian cat or any cat for that matter can be very expensive. This is so because obesity forms the foundation of a wide range of diseases and health conditions that will see you in and out of a vet's clinic on a regular basis. Just like in humans, obesity in cats causes such diseases as arthritis, heart disease, diabetes, cancer of the bladder and breathing difficulty.

The ideal weight of your Abyssinian cat should be between 8-10 pounds (3-4 kg) and between 6-7 pounds (2-3 kg) for a male and female respectively. You need to take anything beyond these as a cause of concern. It is therefore important that you have your cat weighed whenever you visit the vet for regular checkups, which should ideally include weight measurement.

You should be able to tell whether your Aby is becoming obese or not even without weighing it. You should be able to feel your Aby's backbone and ribs whenever you place your hand on its back. Failure to feel the bones should be a clear sign of obesity.

Obesity is a serious health condition in cats. Just like in humans, obesity in cats encourages the occurrence of such serious diseases/health conditions as diabetes, heart disease and cardiovascular diseases. Ensuring that your Aby maintains normal body weight will go a long way in preventing regular trips to a vet's clinic, which translates to reduced health care costs.

Your Aby can become obese for several reasons one of which is free feeding. Most cats left free to choose when to eat often develop obesity. This is so because a free feeding program gives a cat the opportunity to overeat, in effect consuming too much food that its body really needs. Veterinarians recommend feeding your adult Aby between two to three meals in a day with the amounts of each meal controlled to avoid overeating. Ideally, your Aby's food should be about half of a human meal.

The other main cause of obesity in cats is the intake of too many calories. Unlike humans, your Aby does not have the Amylase enzyme that digests carbohydrates contained in their food. The enzyme plays a very important role of breaking down large carbohydrate molecules into smaller absorbable units of glucose. Furthermore, cats are not carbohydrate consumers by their nature. Because most cat dry foods contain high levels of carbohydrates, you need to shop carefully for the same. Any dry cat food you buy must have minimal carbohydrates, if any. It is highly recommended that you feed your Aby a diet that is similar to its natural food, which makes canned cat food better. A cat's ideal diet should be high on meat-based protein and moderate fat and water.

Apart from carbohydrates and free feeding program, the other main cause of obesity in cats is cat treats. Availability of cat treats has made many cat owners lazy when it comes to feeding their cats. Many cat owners rely on cat treats as their cats' main food. Cat treats contain high levels of carbohydrates and feeding them to your Aby on a regular basis puts it at great risk of becoming obese. You should only feed your Aby treats at special occasions as a way of appreciation or reward.

Unlike in humans, obesity in cats is a non-inherited health condition. Your Aby will only develop obesity because of what you feed it. It is therefore very necessary that you pay attention to what your Aby eats and in what amounts.

Apart from food, you seriously need to ensure that your Aby is physically engaged on a daily basis. Exercises are very important not only for your Aby's physique but also in stimulating its mind. You need to make effective use of cat toys to help your Aby burn excess fat deposits in the body.

Formulating a balanced and nutritious weight loss diet should also be effective in helping your Aby cut down on excess body weight just in case it has already become obese. You need to formulate a diet that is low in carbohydrates but high on meat-based protein and other nutrients, including fresh drinking water.

## Pustules

Cat pustules are similar to human acne. Just like in humans who suffer acne mostly on the facial area, your Aby is also likely to suffer acne that affects its chin although its lower lip can also be affected. Major causes of pustules in acne happen to be poor grooming (lack of it) and excess oil on the skin surface, oil produced from within the body.

Just like acne in humans, your Aby is most likely to present such symptoms as black/whiteheads, swollen chin and development of nodules that can be very painful. Your cat can end up having boils as a result of pustules.

A vet will normally try to rule out such health issues as feline leprosy, allergy and skin tumors before diagnosing pustules. Confirmation of correct diagnosis is usually through such procedures as a fungal culture, biopsy test and skin scraping among other procedures.

For treatment, a vet will normally prescribe antibiotics, topical creams and shampoos. Regular occurrence of pustules should be a cause of concern regarding your Aby's general health. It may be necessary for a vet to undertake your Aby's full health scan to ascertain the exact cause of the disease.

## Hypoadrenocorticism

This is what is commonly referred to as Addison's disease, even in humans. This disease is mostly caused by imbalance in the levels of both glucocorticoid (cortisol) and mineralocorticoids (aldosterone) hormones produced in the adrenal gland. These two hormones play a very important role in maintaining your Aby's good health and excess or insufficient production of the same leads to serious health complications. Excess or insufficient production of the two hormones impairs the function of the kidneys, gastrointestinal system, the nervous system and the cardiovascular system.

You Aby will present a number of symptoms that may include signs of depression, vomiting, bloody feces, unexplained weight loss, general body weakness and lack of appetite among other symptoms. Apart from excess or insufficient production of the two hormones, the disease can also be caused by metastatic tumors.

A vet will normally perform elaborate laboratory tests, blood count and urinalysis tests in diagnosing if your Aby suffers from Addison's disease. If so, he/she may recommend that your Aby remains hospitalized for intensive therapy since Addison's disease is usually an emergency case. The first line of treatment is usually the giving of body fluids intravenously with the aim of balancing the two hormones. Your Aby will henceforth need to receive hormonal treatment throughout its life even with recovery.

### Feline Asthma/Bronchitis

This is the inflammation of your Aby's bronchi and bronchioles. The inflammation narrows your Aby's airwaves. Left untreated, asthma/bronchitis presents the risk of your Aby developing excess tissue within its lungs, tissues that make it very difficult for the lungs to inflate.

In both acute and chronic asthma/bronchitis cases, your Aby is most likely to present such symptoms as coughing, body weakness, general body weakness, lack of appetite, breathing difficulties and skin coloration among other symptoms.

Although the exact cause of asthma/bronchitis in cats is yet to be known, your Aby is most likely to suffer the condition if you smoke in the house and your Aby inhales the smoke. The disease has also been linked to parasitic lung infection and in particular infection by lungworm, use of air fresheners at home and indoor chemical sprays.

Diagnosis of asthma/bronchitis in cats is usually through blood tests that also show whether it is acute or chronic. A vet may also need your Aby's fecal sample to ascertain if parasites are present. There are instances when a vet may order an X-ray imaging with the aim of ascertaining both the nature and extent of the disease.

Asthma/bronchitis in cats is usually a serious disease and your Aby will most likely be given oxygen therapy in addition to anti-inflammatory medications to reduce swelling of the airwaves. A vet may recommend that your Aby remains hospitalized for further investigation and monitoring.

### Tyzzer Disease

This is a disease that mostly affects both kittens and young cats. It is a serious life threatening disease caused by Clostridium piliformis bacterium. The bacterium multiplies within the intestines before entering a cat's liver, leading to serious damage of the liver.

If infected, your Aby will show a number of symptoms including general body weakness, signs of depression, loss of appetite, diarrhea, low body temperature and abdominal distension among other symptoms.

Veterinarians do diagnose Tyzzer disease through laboratory tests of blood, urinalysis and blood count among other diagnosis procedures. Diagnosis of the disease is usually revealed when there is high level of liver enzymes. There is no treatment for Tyzzer disease and affected cats do die.

### Capillariasis

This is a cat disease caused by the Capillaria plica and Capillaria feliscati parasitic worms. Although the parasites mostly affect a cat's urinary bladder, it can also affect its urinary tract. Your Aby will most likely show signs of frequent urination that can be painful. Bloody urine and straining when urinating are also symptoms.

Diagnosis of this disease is through urinalysis, which should reveal presence of Capillaria ova. A vet may offer injections or other form of medications for treatment. The possibility of the disease recurring usually remains high especially if your Aby is fond of venturing outdoors often. This is because it is outdoors where it has access to earthworms.

### *Hepatic Lipidosis*

This is a liver disease that is commonly referred to as fatty liver. It is one of the most fatal diseases that affect domestic cats across the world. The liver plays the important roles of synthesizing proteins, producing digestive enzymes and detoxifying the body. By its nature, a cat's liver cannot convert large amounts of fat into energy the way it is in humans. Failure by a cat's liver to convert large amounts of fat efficiently leads to accumulation of fat, which impairs the liver's function. Furthermore, the liver releases the accumulated fat that by then has turned yellow into the bloodstream, leading to yellowish eyes. Left untreated, a cat develops several health complications before dying of the disease.

Various health conditions and diseases including cancer, diabetes, kidney disease, inflammation of the pancreas and obesity, among others, can cause fatty liver. If affected, your Aby will most likely present such symptoms as yellowish eyes, unexplained rapid weight loss, signs of depression, jaundice, vomiting, constipation and drooling of saliva.

A vet will normally perform routine laboratory tests of blood count, urinalysis and biochemistry profile in diagnosing the disease. Such other imaging tools as radiography may also be performed to examine the abdomen. You Aby will most likely be hospitalized for treatment, which includes fluid therapy and vitamin B supplementation. A vet will obviously recommend an appropriate diet for your Aby to prevent re-occurrence of the disease.

### *Sporotrichosis*

This is a disease caused by Sporothrix schenckii fungus found in mold and yeast. Your Aby can easily contract the fungus when it rubs against a surface with mold or yeast, in which case the fungus attaches to its skin before penetrating into the body. Your Aby can also contract the disease when it inhales fumes from molds.

If infected, your Aby will most likely present such symptoms as skin lesions, swollen lymph glands and wounds on the head among other symptoms. This is a zoonotic disease that can be transmitted from human to animals and vice versa. It is therefore very important that you be careful when outdoors with your Aby. In particular, your Aby should not venture into areas with decaying organic matter.

In addition to physical examination, a vet will normally carry out laboratory fluid tests to diagnose the disease. Your Aby will most likely be hospitalized for treatment that includes administration of anti-fungal therapy.

### *Feline Trichobezoars*

This is what is referred to as hairballs. Although it is perfectly normal for your Aby to occasionally vomit a hairball, persistent and frequent vomiting of hairballs is usually a sign of a serious health problem.

The only evidence that your Aby vomits hairballs is when you see the hairballs. These are masses of hair that are cylindrically shaped. They can form in your Aby's stomach and it only vomits them out when it regurgitates.

The cause of hairballs is directly linked to how cats groom themselves. Your Aby's tongue is designed in such a way that it is barbed, which makes it possible for it to groom itself with ease. In the process of grooming itself, it swallows some of the hair it removes. It is this hair that accumulates in the stomach that it vomits or regurgitates.

Frequent vomiting or regurgitation of hairballs calls for veterinary attention. Ideally the vets will perform such tests as blood cell count, biochemistry profile and thyroid screening among other tests to diagnose hairballs.

Hairball treatment usually involves lubricating the hairballs in the stomach to make it easy for a cat to pass them with a bowel movement. A vet can also recommend feeding your Aby some cats foods that are commercially available, foods that control accumulation of hair in the stomach. The best way to prevent your Aby having hairballs is to groom it regularly.

### Polyphagia

Polyphagia simply refers to a cat's increased appetite for food. It is a health condition where your Aby can simply start demanding more food to the extent of becoming ravenous all the time. This condition can be caused by many factors. It is appropriate that you ascertain the exact cause your Aby suddenly starts demanding for more food. Although your Aby may gain weight, weight loss will be a sign that it is not well.

In addition to increased appetite, your Aby will most likely develop obesity or lose weight. Causes include onset of the aging process, use of certain cat medications, diabetes and poor absorption of food.

Polyphagia is normally diagnosed through blood, urine tests and radiography imaging. Treatment normally takes into account the causative factor, which in case of a disease requires that a vet advises on the best management regime while treating the initial disease (causative factor).

### Panosteitis

Panosteitis refers to inflammation of bones in cats. It is a very painful health condition that affects the long bones found in a cat's legs. If affected, your Aby will most likely limp before becoming lame. Although this condition mostly affects large-sized cats, it can also affect your Aby. It is a treatable health condition that a cat can recover from and lead a perfectly normal life.

In addition to limping, your Aby is also most likely to show such other symptoms as signs of depression, fever, anorexia and weight loss among other symptoms. While the actual cause of this health condition remains unknown, diagnosis is through X-ray imaging and blood tests. Treatment of this health condition is usually limited to pain management in which case a vet is bound to prescribe anti-inflammatory and steroid medications.

### Inflammatory Bowel Disease (IBD)

IBD is a term used to refer to several diseases and health conditions that affect a cat's gastrointestinal tract and whose cause(s) remain largely unknown. One characteristic of all the diseases is that they cause inflammation of the intestines.

Your Aby will present several symptoms if affected. Some of these include diarrhea, signs of depression, flatulence, abdominal pain, general body weakness, bloody stool and distressed hair on the coat.

Diagnosis of IBD is normally through laboratory tests including blood count, biochemistry profile and urinalysis. Although a cure for IBD is not available, a vet will normally institute control measures that include stabilization of body weight, reduction of immune system response and administration of antibiotic medications.

### Coprophagia

This is a health condition that normally worries cat owners. Your Aby may suddenly start eating its own feces after defecating. Although the actual cause of this condition is unknown, it is thought to be a result of both mineral and vitamin deficiency in a cat's diet.

Apart from eating its feces, you may also observe your Aby eating rocks, clay and soap among other non-edible items. Your Aby will also have diarrhea and vomit frequently.

Apart from mineral and vitamin deficiency, other factors believed to cause the condition include malnutrition and such other diseases as thyroid disease, diabetes and increased appetite among other factors.

Diagnosing this health condition can be very involving. A vet will normally determine whether the condition is a simple behavioral problem or a medical condition, in which case he/she will undertake a complete biochemistry profile, blood count and urinalysis. Treating this condition depends on causative factors. While changing your Aby's environment may help if the causative factor is ascertained to be behavioral, a vet may prescribe specific medications should the causative factor be medically related.

### Urine Incontinence

This is a case of lack of control of the bladder, just in the same way it is in humans. Your Aby will present different symptoms in case it has this health condition. Such symptoms include frequent urination, wet hair between its rear legs or on the abdomen, skin inflammation around its genitals and wet beddings among other symptoms.

There are many factors that can make your Aby lose control of its bladder. Some of these include neutering/spaying procedures that disrupt the nerves around the bladder, lesions on the brain, overactive bladder syndrome, UTIs, lesions on the spinal cord and underdevelopment of the bladder among many other causes.

Diagnosing urine incontinence in cats can be very challenging because of the many possible causes. A vet will strive to ascertain the particular cause before designing an effective treatment plan that may take some time. Treatment normally depends on the ascertained cause.

### Mesothelioma

Mesothelioma refers to a rare type of tumor that develops on the cellular tissue lining the interior part of a cat's body, the epithelial linings. These linings play an important role of protecting the internal organs by covering them. They also facilitate movement within the body.

Just like with other types of tumors, Mesothelioma develops when mesothelium cells fail to divide or replicate in the normal way before migrating to other parts of the body, which further spreads the tumor.

Your Aby will show several symptoms if affected including difficulty in breathing, muffled lung/heart sounds, general body weakness, vomiting, inability to exercise and enlarged abdomen among other symptoms.

Diagnosing this condition normally involves a vet undertaking a complete blood profile, blood count and urinalysis. A vet may also obtain X-ray image of your Aby's abdomen/chest, radiography and ultrasound to observe presence of masses in the body cavities. Drainage of unnecessary fluids within the body is usually the first line of treatment before medications are prescribed.

### Stertor/Stridor

While Stertor refers to a cat's low-pitched noisy breathing, Stridor refers to the high-pitched noisy breathing that your Aby can exhibit. Stertor is most likely to occur when your Aby inhales air. It is similar to snoring except that your Aby's inhalation of air will be constricted, resulting in a low-pitched breathing occasioned by vibration of tissues that align the throat. On the other hand, Stridor is likely to occur when your Aby inhales air with throat tissues in a rigid state.

Your Aby will exhibit a number of symptoms when affected. These include inability to meow and extra-ordinary nature of breathing among other symptoms. These two related conditions can be caused by narrowed nostrils, inverted laryngeal, paralysis of the voice box/windpipe, tumor of the voice box and presence of foreign matter within the windpipe.

There are also risk factors associated with occurrence of the two health conditions. Some of these include an environment with high temperatures, high metabolic rate, over-exercising and poor drinking/eating habits among other possible risk factors.

Diagnosis of the two conditions usually involves a vet obtaining your Aby's health history, performing internal imaging procedures (fluoroscopy) and X-ray imaging of the neck to identify any abnormalities in the neck's soft tissues. There are instances where a vet may need to perform surgery when foreign matter is lodged within the windpipe.

### Baylisascarisis

This is what is referred to as Raccoon disease in cats. The disease also affects humans. It is transmitted by larvae of the Baylisascarisis procyyonis parasite (roundworm), found in feces left open in the environment. Your Aby is most likely to contract the larvae in case it is used to venturing outdoors into areas with other cats having the parasite.

Your Aby will present several symptoms if affected. These include uncoordinated walking, difficulty in swallowing, regular seizures and general confusion among other symptoms.

Diagnosis of this disease is through laboratory examination of a fecal smear test that should detect the presence of the disease in your Aby's intestines. The larvae should be seen through ophthalmoscopic examination. There are a good number of medications that a vet can prescribe for your Aby, including Corticosteroids and albendazole medications.

## Idiopathic Epilepsy

This is seizures in cats. It is a disorder that occurs in a cat's brain and causes sudden and, in almost cases, uncontrolled/recurring attacks. If affected, your Aby may or may not lose consciousness. Your Aby will normally have a short aura and look as if it is under threat. Your Aby will eventually fall on its side at the onset of attack and may salivate, defecate or urinate. An attack can last between 20 and 90 seconds before it recovers.

Although seizures may occur when your Aby is awake, the same can occur when it is asleep. The period soon after an attack is usually followed by such behavior as general confusion, blindness, increased thirst, increased appetite and aimless wondering among other abnormal behaviors.

The exact cause(s) of idiopathic epilepsy remains largely unknown although it has been proved to be a hereditary health condition. Diagnosis of the condition normally involves blood cell count, thyroid screening and testing for viral infections if any. Treatment of this condition normally involves administration of anticonvulsant medications.

## Accidents

Although all cats are susceptible to accidents, Abyssinians are very prone to the same. This is simply because of their playful nature and the fact that they like heights. This is why it is very important that you make your home as cat friendly as possible by removing any sharp objects on the floor. Serious injuries require that you take your cat to a vet at the earliest possible time since these can be life threatening.

## Signs of Illness

Diseases do not develop overnight. It takes time before your cat finally falls ill. You need to be able to notice when your cat starts to show abnormal behavior even before she falls ill. You can only do this if you interact and socialize with your cat to a point where you can easily tell when it is about to fall ill.

Signs of illness in cats can be categorized into two: behavioral and physical signs.

### *Behavioral Signs*

You should be able to notice different unusual behaviors by your cat, behaviors that should prompt you to take your cat to a vet at the earliest possible opportunity unless you know the reason for a behavior.

Although your cat will avoid its litter box when the box is unclean, avoidance of the same is usually a clear sign of a medical condition. Urination outside the litter box can be a sign of such medical conditions as diabetes, urinary tract infection or kidney failure. You need to take your cat to a vet in case you notice this unusual behavior more than once when the litter box is perfectly clean.

Cats generally are not fond of drinking water. They obtain the water they need from their food. Although your cat will occasionally drink water, increased intake of water should be a cause of concern. This will be a sign of thirst, which is usually a sign of such health conditions/diseases as diabetes and hyperthyroidism among other diseases.

Failure by your cat to eat as it normally does should be a serious cause of concern. This may be an indication of loss of appetite that may in turn be a sign of many diseases including gingivitis, trauma or anemia among many other diseases.

Interacting and socializing with your cat should make it possible for you to know when and why it meows. Excess meowing (vocalization) may be a sign of stress, fear, sickness, pain or other medical conditions.

Your Abyssinian cat is most likely to spend a better part of the day sleeping, particularly during the morning hours. Although this is perfectly normal, excessive sleep in addition to hiding when it is awake should be a sign of fear, anxiety or sickness.

Being people-oriented, your Aby will most likely get into the habit of welcoming you whenever you arrive at home. You will need to be concerned with any change in this habit. You will need to establish where your cat goes when not welcoming you. It is most likely that you will find your cat in its litter box, which should alert you of a medical problem.

### *Physical Signs*

Unlike behavioral signs of sickness, physical signs are easy to notice and one of the most obvious signs you should be able to notice is a change in your cat's coat appearance. The fact that cats generally groom themselves means that your cat's coat should always be smooth. You should be concerned when the coat appears ruffled, which may be a sign of malnutrition, parasitic infection or such other skin disorders as ringworm, or allergy.

Your Aby should always have good breath. Bad breath will definitely not be normal since such may be a sign of diabetes, gingivitis, kidney disease or gastrointestinal disorder among other diseases/health conditions.

Any rapid weight loss or gain should be a serious concern. This is so because such may be a sign of many health conditions including malnutrition, overfeeding, diabetes, kidney failure or heart disease among many others.

## When to Visit a Vet

Regardless of your Aby's age, five very important factors determine how healthy it will be: proper nutrition and weight management, environment, good dental care, parasite control and vaccinations. The foods that you feed your Aby determine whether it will remain healthy throughout its lifetime. You also need to make your cat's environment as friendly as possible to allow your Aby to enjoy its life to the fullest. Ensure that you do not only socialize with your Aby but engage in play activities as well.

Ensuring that your Aby's oral health is at its optimum will also go a long way in preventing many diseases. Closely related to environment is the issue of parasites. Note that parasites thrive in unhygienic locations and it is therefore very necessary to ensure that your cat's room or space remains clean all the time. Lastly, you need to ensure that your Abyssinian cat receives all the recommended vaccinations and any other vaccination administered by relevant authorities.

When to take your cat to a vet depends on its age. Although kittens are in most cases sold off when they have already received the most important vaccinations, you will need to take yours to a vet at least three times a year for any additional vaccinations or routine checkups. Doing so will make it possible for you to know any health issues that your kitten may have once it comes of age.

An adult Aby does not require too much vet attention so long as you feed it recommended foods and keep its environment clean. Your adult Aby will have received the recommended vaccinations and should be in a position to remain healthy for a long time. You will however need to take it to a vet at least twice a year for routine checkups.

Having an old or aging Aby can be a little of a problem because of the many visits you may need to make to a vet clinic. This is because it is during old age that such age-related diseases/health

conditions such as arthritis and heart disease among others set in.
You will need to take your aging Aby to a vet at least three times
in a year for routine medical checkups and for such indicated
diseases/health conditions.

Your Aby's general health remains squarely in your hands. You
should take every step possible to ensure that your Aby is not at
risk of contracting any disease. You should be in a position to
perform at-home physical examinations on a regular basis with
the aim of determining your Aby's health condition.

Although you need to take your kitten, cat or aging cat to a vet as
indicated, there are instances when it becomes necessary to take it
to a vet at the earliest opportunity possible. Such incidents as
accidents require that you take your Aby to a vet for immediate
medical attention.

## The Veterinarian

The professionals commonly referred to as veterinarians or vets in
short are actually veterinary physicians trained to treat diseases,
disorders and injuries that affect non-human animals. Vets are
referred to differently in different countries around the world.
Although they are generally referred to as vets, they are
professionally referred to as veterinary surgeons in the UK for
instance.

Different countries have strict legislation when it comes to
veterinary services, just the same way it is with human
physicians. It is mandatory in almost all countries for anyone
titled as a vet to have undertaken the necessary training,
registered and licensed to practice as a vet. Vets work in many
institutions. There are those that work in vet clinics where they
engage with animal owners or pet owners directly in treating their
livestock. There are also those that work in such institutions as
zoos, research institutions and animal hospitals.

Just in the same way that human doctors specialize in a specific area, vets also specialize. You are therefore most likely to come across a vet who is a surgery or dermatology specialist or one specializing in internal medicine. Generally, vets diagnose and treat non-human diseases and health conditions in addition to providing aftercare and administration of vaccines.

It is common practice to find vets in different countries working in the private sector. Only a small number work in government institutions. The fact that the majority work in the private sector and in particular in clinics allows them to work directly with animal owners, owners whose animals have varied diseases and health conditions.

The fact that you plan to buy or already own a cat and an Abyssinian cat for that matter will obviously make it necessary to pay a vet a visit. This can be on the first day when you bring your Aby home for the requisite vaccine(s). Just like with choosing your personal physician, you need to carefully choose a vet to attend to your Aby's treatment and administration of vaccines.

## How to Find a Good Vet

The fact that most vets work in clinics, and private clinics at that, can make finding the best vet a big challenge. This can be very true when you live in a location where there are many practicing vets. The first way to finding the right vet is to enquire from close family members, neighbors and friends with pets. They should be able to refer you to a vet they personally know and who provides quality service.

Apart from making enquiries, you also have the option of consulting your local professional organization for information on licensed vets practicing in your locality. You also have the option of getting information on the right vets from a local cat breeder. A breeder in particular will be better placed to refer you to the right vet because he/she obviously engages a vet to treat his/her cats in the cattery.

Whether you choose to make enquiries or contact a professional organization or a cat breeder, there are certainly several issues you will need to ascertain before you engage the services of a vet and one of these issues is whether the vet is licensed and is accredited. A professional and ethical vet will normally share with you his certification, which should ideally be posted on the wall. You will also need to ascertain whether the vet is a member of a local professional organization.

Apart from a vet's certification, accreditation and level of experience, you need to undertake an overall assessment of the facility with knowledge that it is at that clinic where you will be bringing your Aby in case of health problems. It is therefore important to assess a facility's level of cleanliness among other issues.

It is common for vets to enter into agreements with pet owners for the purpose of taking care of their pets' health. Although most pet owners are in favor of such agreements as one way of cutting down on their pets' health care costs, doing so can be costly without due diligence. It is possible that you and your pet's vet can have disagreements that force you to engage the services of a different vet. Terminating an agreement can be very costly depending on the agreement period. The best way to cut down on your Aby's health care costs is to shop for a suitable pet insurance policy that covers risks to which your Aby is susceptible.

## Cat Insurance

Your Abyssinian cat is not only people friendly; it turns out to be the best companion you can have at home as a pet. Furthermore, it makes you active because of its playful nature. It is definitely a valuable family member. Just in the same way that you ensure your other family members are comfortable and in good health, you need to ensure that your Aby also remains in good health and one way to go about this is to take out cat insurance for your Aby.

It is a fact that veterinary fees and medication costs are always on the rise, which can make it impossible for you to meet your Aby's medical costs at a time it needs it most. Taking out appropriate cat insurance policy goes a long way in keeping your veterinary costs low while giving your cat good health care.

Regardless of your location, any cat insurance policy you are likely to find is designed to cover the cost of veterinary fees and treatment of diseases/health conditions and injuries. Although very important, choosing the right cat insurance policy for your Aby can be a big challenge. This is because there are simply many policies out there in the market that differ in terms of what they cover and price. This makes it necessary to know the best time to take out cat insurance.

The best time to take out cat insurance is when your cat is young, a kitten. This is because age is one of the most important factors pet insurance companies take into consideration when determining the level of insurance premium to quote. Kittens generally attract low premium rates compared to adult and aging cats that attract high premium rates because of various factors including the onset of age-related diseases/health conditions.

There are generally four types of cat insurance policies you can choose from: lifetime, maximum benefit, limited-time and accident-only policies.

Lifetime cat insurance policies cover vet fees for one year. You will need continuous renewal of the policy to enjoy the same coverage at the same premium rate regardless of how many claims you make. Although the cost of this policy is usually on the higher side, it is beneficial taking into account the fact that your Aby remains covered for its lifetime even when it develops life-long disease.

Unlike the lifetime policy, the maximum benefit policy provides coverage for a pre-determined maximum amount of veterinary fees per health condition. The specific health condition is considered a pre-existing condition and is therefore excluded from future claims once the maximum limit is reached.

The time-limited policy is similar to the maximum benefit policy except that the latter is limited to one year only, a period in which vet fees can be offset for each health condition.

The accident-only policy is limited to treatment of injuries your Aby may sustain from accidents at home or outside the home including on the road.

A common feature of almost all cat insurance policies is the exclusion of pre-existing medical conditions. Other procedures such as preventative treatments, pregnancy/birth, neutering/spaying and worm control are also excluded from the policies. It is very important that you undertake a little research with the aim of finding a pet insurance company that quotes low premium rates on policies that provide a specific coverage you need for your Aby.

# Chapter 11 – Vaccinations

## What is a Vaccine?

A vaccine is basically a solution containing antigens that to the body's immune system looks like disease-causing organisms, but are not. Your Aby can be given a vaccine orally or through injection. When introduced into the body, the vaccine stimulates the body's complex immune system, making the system strong enough to fight any disease-causing organism that enters the body. Having your Aby vaccinated is therefore very important.

Different jurisdictions have different vaccine requirements for all pets, including cats. While some vaccines are only available in particular regions of the world because of the prevalence of specific cat diseases, others are only available in other regions. There are basically two types of vaccines: core and non-core vaccines. While core vaccines are mandatory to all cats regardless of region or location, non-core vaccines are only found in specific regions or locations.

Like with anything introduced into the body, vaccines present several symptoms including fever, vomiting, loss of appetite, sluggishness, diarrhea and swelling around injection area. There are also serious symptoms that may occur depending on the kind of vaccine your cat receives. These include life-threatening allergic reactions and development of tumors around injected area. The serious symptoms are limited in occurrence. Vaccine symptoms are generally mild and do fade away within a few days.

## Safety of Vaccines

Although cat vaccines are generally safe, there has been controversy around some vaccines that are often considered unnecessary. You need to appreciate the fact that it is because of feline vaccines that cats can now live beyond their expected lifespan. Production and administration of most vaccines that had raised controversies have luckily ceased. It is therefore perfectly safe to take your Aby to a vet to receive the core vaccines.

One major challenge that many cat owners face is when to have their cats vaccinated. There are different circumstances and instances when your Aby needs to be vaccinated.

## Kitten Vaccination

Your Abyssinian kitten or cat is most likely to have received its first vaccination while still with the breeder from whom you bought it. Even so, the vaccination must have been several weeks after it was born. This is because kittens naturally acquire sufficient immunity from their mothers through milk. Furthermore, a kitten's immune system is still not yet fully developed to receive artificial vaccination.

Breeders arrange with veterinarians for their kittens to be vaccinated once they attain the age of seven weeks with additional vaccinations administered when they are twelve and again when they attain the age of sixteen years. The two additional vaccinations are in most cases boosters that fortify the first vaccination.

## Adult Cat Immunization

Adult cats are not vaccinated but rather immunized. Like with vaccination, immunization is aimed at further boosting your Aby's immune system to continue being effective in offering protection against possible infections.

## Core Cat Vaccines

Core cat vaccines are those that all cats should receive regardless of location. These vaccines are very effective in offering protection against life-threatening diseases found in all regions of the world. They include:

### *Feline Viral Rhinotracheitis (FVR) Vaccine*

FVR Vaccine is administered to protect against FVR virus that is at times referred to as feline influenza or feline pneumonia. This is a respiratory disease found across the globe.

FVR is a highly contagious disease that can kill kittens within a few days of infection. The disease is easily transmitted through direct contact. One cat passes the disease on to another cat through saliva, nasal and eye secretions. When infected, your Aby will most likely show such signs as coughing, sneezing, excessive nasal discharge, loss of appetite and high fever.

### *Feline Calicivirus (FCV) Vaccine*

Your Aby receives this vaccination to protect itself against the virus that causes respiratory infection. Occurrence of this disease usually ends in epidemic in areas with large cat populations because of its highly contagious nature.

FCV presents such symptoms as nose/eye discharge, mouth ulceration, anorexia and general body weakness at the initial stage. If affected, your Aby is likely to present secondary symptoms such as jaundice, high fever, swelling of the face and limbs (edema) and dysfunction of organs within the body.

### *Feline Panleukopenia Virus (FPV) Vaccine*

FPV vaccine is one of the most important cat vaccines that your cat must receive. This is because the vaccine offers protection against the highly contagious and fatal diseases caused by

Panleukopenia virus that causes low white blood cells. The disease is largely transmitted through contact with body fluids of an affected cat.

If infected, your Aby is most likely to show signs of severe dehydration, bloody diarrhea, anemia, depression, vomiting, loss of appetite, self-biting and loss of skin elasticity among other signs. Pregnant cats affected by the disease give birth to kittens with cerebellar hypopasia.

### *Feline Immunodeficiency Virus (FIV) Vaccine*

FIV is often referred to as feline AIDS. This is so because it is in many ways similar to human immunodeficiency virus (HIV) in human beings. There are several different types of FIV that the FIV Vaccine is designed to protect against. Like in humans, your Aby is most likely to live with FIV in case of infection in which case it will now be a carrier of the virus.

FIV attacks the immune system just in the same way that HIV does in humans. Although FIV and HIV are similar, humans cannot contract FIV and cats cannot contract HIV. Should your cat be infected, it will henceforth transmit the virus to other cats through saliva. Outdoor cats happen to be more at risk of contracting FIV virus compared to indoor cats.

## Non-Core Cat Vaccines

Although classified as non-core cat vaccines, vaccines in this category are core in some regions of the world. This is because they are designed to offer cats protection against specific diseases only found in such regions. They include:

### *Feline Leukemia Virus (FLV) Vaccine*

FLV is a virus that causes life-threatening diseases in cats. One common disease associated with the virus is leukemia, which develops when the virus destroys blood cells, in effect making them cancerous. The virus presents several symptoms including loss of appetite, poor coat condition, skin infections, fatigue, oral infections including gingivitis, diarrhea and jaundice among many other symptoms. Your Aby, if infected, will be able to transmit the virus to other cats through saliva, litter box (sharing) and food/water dishes.

### Rabies Vaccine

Rabies was in the past a universal medical condition that affected humans, dogs and other warm-blooded animals such as cats. Vaccination campaigns undertaken in specific regions of the world made it possible for the disease to be eradicated in such regions. Rabies vaccine is now only common in specific regions where cats, dogs and humans can still be infected.

Rabies is a serious disease that you should protect your Aby against through vaccination, depending on your region. It is a viral disease that causes serious inflammation of the brain. It presents such symptoms as fever, loss of consciousness and restricted movement among other symptoms. Most rabies cases do result in death.

### Chlamydophila Felis Vaccine

Chlamydophila felis is a bacteria commonly found in cats. The vaccine for the bacteria is designed to protect against it. The bacteria cause inflammation of a cat's conjunctiva, rhinitis and respiratory health problems.

Depending on your jurisdiction, you may be required from time to time to take your cat to a local vet for specific vaccinations aimed at preventing identified cat diseases in your specific area. Such vaccinations are in most cases occasioned by outbreak of cat diseases. Different countries have legislations that make such vaccinations mandatory and failure to adhere to the same attracts different consequences.

Apart from being a requirement of legislation, you need to consider your cat's vaccination seriously. This is because you are the ultimate beneficiary knowing that your cat is fully vaccinated or immunized and therefore well protected from diseases that can affect its health. It is therefore very important that you consult your local vet on a regular basis for proper information on cat vaccinations and immunizations.

# Chapter 12 – Costs

## Estimated Monthly/Yearly Maintenance Costs

Owning an Abyssinian cat is very fulfilling. Not only is it a pet but a valuable companion as well. However, being responsible for your lovely Aby comes at a cost, which you are obligated to bear. Maintaining a cat can be very expensive, if you choose to be committed in meeting its demands and needs.

You should be capable of maintaining your Aby to make it different from any other Aby on the street. Failure to meet some of your Aby's needs and demands can easily be a cause of health problems. Furthermore, you stand the risk of losing your cat since it may simply run away into the street.

There are different costs you are bound to incur when you plan to own and maintain an Abyssinian. You are most likely to incur heavy expenses when you prepare to buy or adopt an Abyssinian cat. Most of the costs relate to supplies that your Aby will need soon after arriving at home. They include:

**Food** – There is no doubt that your Aby will need to eat not just any food but quality cat food. This will be a reoccurring expense since you will need to buy quality food often. The cost of quality cat food averages $120 - £71 and -$150 - £89 per month depending on your location. Yearly maintenance costs on food will therefore be around $1,800 - £ 1,072 in any given year.

**Nutrition Supplements** – These are dietary supplements that you may need to buy for your Aby. You will need to consult with a vet before buying any. Ideally, the vet should inform you when your Aby needs supplements, which may be because of special needs. You may need to incur about $100 - £60 at any given time on dietary supplements.

**Food/Water Bowls** – These are supplies you will need to buy before you bring your Aby home. Note that sharing of food/water bowls used by your Aby will not be allowed. For instance, you should not feed your dog on the same food/water bowls used by your Aby. Quality food/water bowls retail between $10 - £6 and $30 - £17.80 depending on your location. Note that you may need to replace the same at least twice in any given year, which makes yearly costs on food/water bowls between $60 - £35 and $90 - £54.

**Treats** – Treats are edibles that you will need to feed your Aby once in a while. They are actually niceties that you use as rewards when your Aby does something positive. You are most likely to offer your Aby treats more often during the first few months as you subject it to training, in which case you are bound to incur between $30 - £17.80 and $100 - £60 every month. Yearly treat costs average between $60 - £35 and $300 - £178.

**Grooming Supplies** – Like with all cats, your Aby is naturally a clean cat that goes the extra mile to keep itself as clean as possible. It will therefore groom itself often to achieve this. You will still need to groom your cat, in which case you will be obligated to invest in quality grooming supplies. While you are bound to spend between $50 - £ 30 and $100 - £60 in buying permanent grooming supplies such as tools, you will spend between $30 - £17.80 and $60 - £35 on such other recurrent supplies as shampoos and odor removers every month. Your Aby's grooming costs will average between $200 - £120 and $500 - £300.

**Cat Bed** – Your Aby will need a good place to sleep in and investing in a quality cat bed is highly recommended. A cat bed lasts a long time and you may only need to replace it when it is very necessary. A quality cat bed retails at around $20 - £12 and $100 - £60 depending on your location.

**Cat Carrier** – Like human babies, you will need to invest in a quality cat carrier for use in transporting your Aby. Cats are generally not fond of traveling in cars and having a carrier will make traveling with your Aby trouble-free. A quality cat carrier will set you back an amount between $20 - £12 and $100 - £60. You may only need to replace it after two or three years.

**Cat Toys** – Your Aby is a playful and very active pet. This is why investing in quality cat toys is highly recommended. Having toys around will not only engage your Aby in play but will also go a long way in helping it release a lot of energy, energy that if it would not use will make living with your cat a little bit of a problem. Quality cat toys retail at between $20 - £12 and $50 - £30 each and since you will need to buy different types, you should be ready to spend anything between $100 - £60 and $250 - £150 on toys once in a long time.

**Scratching Post** – Having a cat at home presents the risk of having your furniture scratched. This is because cats have a natural instinct to scratch whenever they feel like doing so. The best way of dealing with the risk is providing your cat with a scratching post, which costs between $50 - £30 and $100 - £60 only once.

Proper care of your Aby is not limited to making food and the other supplies available. You also need to ensure that your Aby is in good health. Veterinary service will therefore be very necessary, at a cost. There are different veterinary services your Aby requires. They include:

**Routine vet exams** – These are routine vet exams a vet will undertake with the aim of determining your Aby's health condition. This can be three times in a year for a kitten, twice for an adult cat and three times for an aging cat. You will be obligated to incur between $50 - £30 and $200 - £120 for such exams in any given year depending on your Aby's age.

**Vaccinations** – Although you are most likely to adopt or buy a vaccinated Aby, there are immunizations it will need to receive once it comes of age. Such immunizations cost between $50 - £30 and $150 - £90 per year.

**Spaying/Neutering** – You may choose to have your Aby spayed/neutered, in which case it will not be able to bring forth offspring. Having your Aby spayed/neutered will cost you between $150 - £89 and $300 - £180, a one-time expense.

**Emergency Care** – You certainly will not rule out your Aby getting injured, which will require emergency vet care. Depending on the nature of the injury and your location, you are most likely to incur between $500 - £300 and $2,000 - £1,190on emergency care, which may involve surgery.

Veterinary costs can be huge to the extent that they exceed any other cat maintenance expenses. This is why many cat owners choose to buy cat insurance policies that cover risks that their cats are exposed to, something which you too may consider.

Maintaining your Aby requires that you be ready to commit yourself financially for its overall well-being and health. On average, your monthly maintenance cost will be between $400 - £238 and $700 - £416 monthly and between $1,500 - £890 and $5,000 - £2980 in a year.

Maintaining a cat can indeed be a very expensive undertaking. There are however several ways through which you can cut down on maintenance expenses and one of these is buying cat food in bulk. You can cut on cat food expenses by almost 50% by simply buying in bulk. The best way of realizing this is to buy in wholesale price, which guarantees you an attractive discount.

Apart from cat food, cat treatment is the other recurrent expenditure you are most likely to incur throughout your cat's life. Taking your cat whenever it is sick or when it becomes injured and paying out of pocket can be very expensive. You need to consider taking out the best cat insurance for your cat. It will be appropriate to shop for a cat insurance policy that covers most of the diseases and health conditions to which your cat is susceptible.

It is not mandatory to buy your cat's equipment, including toys. You can effectively make use of locally available materials to make such equipment like a scratch post, cat bed, cat tree and food/water dishes. You can make these as DIY projects or engage the services of a local artist to make them for you at a very minimal cost.

# Chapter 13 – Care for an Aging Abyssinian Cat

Major milestones have been realized in the last decade or so when it comes to treatment of cat diseases and management of cat health conditions. Improvements of existing cat medications and discovery of new cat treatment methods has made it possible for cats to live much longer than their expected lifespan.

Although all cats of all ages benefit from such improvements, aging cats are the biggest beneficiaries. This is because properly cared for aging cats can now age gracefully without necessarily experiencing the pain and a lot of discomfort that aging cats hitherto experienced in the past.

Although your Abyssinian cat has a lifespan of 12 years, it can live to attain the age of 18 years so long as you provide it with proper care including veterinary care.

## What is Aging?

Aging is a process that every living being goes through. It is a natural process that sets in when life expectancy is attained, which in this case is 12 years for Abyssinian cats. One day in a cat's life is a very long time taking into account the fact that a year in a cat's life is similar to about 15 years for humans. Likewise, a cat aged 15 years is similar to a human being aged 85 years. Just like in humans, the onset of aging in cats brings with it several challenges, some which can make your Aby very uncomfortable if you do not offer the necessary help.

## Physiological & Behavioral Changes

Your Aby will exhibit many changes once it attains old age. One of the most visible changes is the tendency to walk on its hocks. This is because its hind leg muscles become weak to a point where running and jumping becomes difficult. This is the time to change its bed to a larger one because it finds it difficult to curl up in a small bed.

Your aging Aby will also be very forgetful. It may choose to remain outdoors when it ventures out regardless of the weather. This is also the time when your Aby can easily get lost when it is used to venturing out.

A visible sign of aging in cats is usually what is referred to as winding down. This is when it grows thinner with its hip, shoulder and backbones becoming visible. In addition to becoming thinner, the fat layer just under the skin also melts away, further exposing the bones. You at this stage need to consult a vet for advice on special types of cat food and dietary supplements to feed your Aby.

The aging process also causes many faculty changes in your Aby's life. Its hearing and cognition abilities diminish to a great extent. Furthermore, its metabolic rate also declines. In case your Aby is not used to venturing outdoors, it is bound to feel cold most of the time. It is your responsibility to ensure that your Aby sleeps in warm bedding in addition to taking it out to receive sunshine when it is possible.

One fact you need to remember when your Aby ages is the fact that its immunity reduces, making it highly susceptible to many infections. It becomes very necessary to take your Aby to a vet whenever you notice any strange behavior or symptoms for immediate vet care.

Although Abyssinians are generally people-oriented pets, your aging Aby will seek more attention when it ages. This is because it naturally knows that it is incapacitated in many ways and will want to be near you most of the time for comfort and assurance. Your Aby will tend to sleep for longer intervals.

Because of the many behavioral and physiological changes that your Aby goes through once the aging process sets in, it is most likely to engage less in physical activities. It is very important that you exercise your Aby's mind. Limited physical exercise is also necessary to help your cat overcome any discomfort it may experience because of such diseases as arthritis, to which aging cats are highly susceptible.

## Health Challenges in Old Cats

Your aging Aby experiences a lot of changes, including reduced immunity. This exposes it to many diseases/health conditions that you must take note of with the aim of helping it cope. Some of the health challenges your Aby is most likely to face include:

### Parasite Infestation

Your aging Aby will probably not groom itself as it used to do. This exposes it to parasite infestation and in particular ticks and fleas. This will likely happen if it is used to going outdoors. Infestation of these parasites will easily lead to skin infections. The likelihood of your Aby becoming anemic also becomes high. This is when it becomes necessary to use flea spray or powder. Although you have the alternative of using flea collars, they have the disadvantage of being ineffective. Furthermore, flea collars can also cause allergic reactions.

Your Aby is also likely to have internal parasites if it is used to going outdoors, just in the same way it used to do when it was a kitten. It becomes necessary for your aging Aby to receive treatment for worms and in particular roundworms after every three months.

## Blindness

In addition to such health challenges as hearing loss and loss of memory, a major challenge that your aging Aby is likely to face is blindness. This starts as partial loss of vision before developing into total blindness.

Although you may not be able to know when your Aby is losing its vision, there are specific signs you need to look out for. These include reluctance to move, misjudging of heights, clumsiness, eye rubbing, large pupils and when your Aby is easily startled. Because treating blindness due to old age is simply impossible, the best you can do to help your Aby cope is ensure that it moves in a secure environment, offer help all the time and speaking to it often.

## Pain

Such diseases/health conditions like arthritis that your aging Aby is susceptible to are usually accompanied with pain. Your Aby may tremble, shiver or crouch. It becomes very important to understand your Aby's body language with the aim of offering help. It becomes necessary to take your cat to a vet for proper diagnosis of existing disease and appropriate pain medications.

## Dental Infections

Old cats are highly susceptible to dental infections. Indeed about 70% of all old cats suffer from dental infections mostly caused by formation of plaque. It is during your cat's old age that you must ensure that it receives regular dental care. This involves removal of plaque that forms tartar, which in effect leads to gingivitis.

## Arthritis

Arthritis is the most common health problem that cats with old age suffer from, just like in humans. This health condition is usually accompanied by joint pain, pain that can make your cat very uncomfortable. Your cat will find it very difficult to engage in physical activities. The best way to help your cat cope is to consult with a local vet for the best supplements to buy, supplements that support the rebuilding of joint cartilage.

### *Reduced Heart Function*

Just like in humans, your cat's heart function reduces once old age sets in. Its heart muscles do not only weaken but also enlarge. It becomes necessary to take your cat to a vet for regular checkups and medications that strengthen its heart muscles.

# Chapter 14 – What To Do with an Old Cat

Living with an old cat or Abyssinian for that matter can be a serious challenge, especially if it becomes senile. You simply cannot cope with the amount of care it needs to continue living comfortably. It is because of this that you may look for alternative ways on how your Aby can still receive proper care until when it dies. You have three options:

## Cat Rescue Center

Taking your aged Aby to a dedicated cat rescue center may be your only option of letting your aged Aby go. Although it can be very difficult, doing so will lessen your burden of having to watch over your Aby all the time.

Cat rescue centers are institutions established by such organizations as animal welfare societies. Such centers are usually staffed with qualified pet personnel with the necessary skill to take care of pets of all ages. In addition to admitting aged pets, including cats at a small fee, they also offer younger pets for adoption. Rescue centers include rescued pets or those born in such institutions.

Cat rescue centers are funded by donations received from pet lovers and other organizations. Some well-established cat rescue centers serve as educational institutions where pet lovers have the opportunity to learn more about pets they are interested in buying or adopting.

Taking your Aby to a cat rescue center does not mean that they will be euthanized. Most rescue centers allow owners to visit their aged cats, a good opportunity to reconnect with pets they have lived with for a long time.

## Euthanasia

Euthanasia is the other route or option you have when it comes to dealing with your old Abyssinian cat. Most cat owners whose cats are aged choose to have their cats euthanized instead of taking them to cat rescue centers. The main reason for this is the fact that having their cats euthanized eliminates the worry they would otherwise continuously have over their pets at such centers.

Simply put, euthanasia is the practice where life is ended. You may choose to have your aged Aby euthanized in order to relieve it from the pain, anguish, suffering and discomfort it goes through as it waits for its natural death. Different jurisdictions have different laws relating to euthanasia in both humans and pets. Your vet should be in a good position to enlighten you on what laws apply in your jurisdiction.

Just like in the case of humans, a vet will normally require that you sign a consent form before your Aby is euthanized. The signing of the form absolves a vet from any claim you make thereafter that he/she caused your Aby's death. There is however certain instances where vets request pet owners for permission to euthanize their aged pets. Such cases are usually when vets discover serious diseases in the cause of treating cats. Even in such situations, cat owners have the last word on whether their cats should be euthanized.

Whether you take your cat to a vet clinic to be euthanized or call a vet to undertake the procedure at home, the procedure is the same. The procedure normally involves giving an over-dose of anesthesia into the main vein in one of its forelegs. In the case of a difficult or troublesome cat, a crush cage is normally used.

Injection of anesthesia leads to immediate unconsciousness followed by slow death. Your Aby is most likely to exhale and pass urine as body muscles relax after death. To ensure that your

Aby is indeed dead, a vet may give additional injection of anesthesia into the kidney or the heart. Your lovely Aby will most likely die with eyes open and a vet will simply close the eyes before placing the cat in a position where it appears to be just asleep. It is only after this that a vet wraps your Aby in a black bag for both safety and privacy before handing you the cat.

Watching your Aby die can be a very traumatizing experience. The experience can remain in your mind for a very long time. This is why some cat owners choose to remain in a separate room when a vet undertakes euthanasia on their aged cats and other pets.

Most cat owners do choose to call a vet to perform the procedure in their homes rather than at a vet's clinic, a move that you too may consider. This is because having the procedure undertaken at home is somehow less traumatic.

The cost of euthanasia varies from one region to another and from one vet to another. The cost can actually be on the higher side if you choose to call a vet to undertake the procedure at home. Generally, the cost ranges between $30 - £17 and $60 - £35 across the world. It is always recommended that you settle any outstanding amount with a vet before he/she undertake the procedure. This is because you may not find it comfortable talking about payments when your Aby is already dead.

## Home Care

You may choose not to take your aged Aby to a cat rescue center or have it euthanized. You may take this route if you are fond of your Aby and have the time to provide it with all the necessary care it needs until it dies a natural death. Although most cat owners choose to care for their cats at home until they die, the suffering, pain and anguish they go through can be traumatizing.

## Body Disposal

Taking your aged Aby to a cat rescue center may eliminate your responsibility to dispose the body when it finally dies. This will depend on the agreement between you and center management. Most centers do undertake to dispose of the bodies of dead cats. Depending on your arrangement, you may be informed. Having your cat euthanized at a vet's clinic, at home or if you choose to care for your cat at home, you will have to determine how to dispose of the body.

## Burial

Burial of pets is fast becoming popular around the world and it is highly possible that you too may choose to bury your Aby once it is dead. Even so, you need to acquaint yourself with your local by-laws that relate to disposal of dead pet bodies. You will need to bury your Aby before it putrefies, unless you have a freezer where you can store the body for a few days. You may choose to bury your Aby in your back garden or at your local authority's pet cemetery.

Even so, there are instances when you may not be allowed to bury your Aby. Such are instances include a degree of risk to human health. This may apply if your Aby dies of rabies.

## Cremation

Like with burial, cremation is another popular way of disposing dead bodies. You may choose to have the body of your Aby cremated to give you the opportunity to bring its ashes home in a jar to scatter in its room/space or simply keep. It is common to find pet cemeteries having pet cremation facilities where you can have your cat cremated.

## Taxidermy

You may choose to have your Aby treated by a taxidermist, to at least allow you have it at home, although in a static state. Taxidermy is a process where a professional taxidermist removes all your Aby's internal organs including tissue and bones. The remaining skin is then stuffed to make your dead Aby look real.

## Desiccation

At times referred to as freeze-drying, desiccation is the process where water is removed from your Aby's body. Your Aby will simply be put in the right posture before being desiccated. The process can take as long as six months and most cat owners do like the result because of its lifelike nature. Because of environmental factors, the desiccated body is usually housed in a glass container for preservation.

## Resin Preservation

This is another way you may choose to dispose of your dead Aby's body. It involves removal of blood and other body fluids, which are replaced with resin. Resin has the characteristic of setting in solid, which in effect yields a lifelike body.

## Post-Disposal Period

The period soon after disposing of your Aby can be a very trying time. It can indeed by a trying time in case you have other Abyssinians at home. Do cats have feelings? Will they realize that one of them is missing? How will they cope knowing that one of them is missing? It is a fact that cats have feelings. Abyssinians in particular develop strong bonds. They will be troubled with the absence of one of them.

One thing you may notice when you have two Abyssinians as pets is that each of them marks its own territory. One of them naturally becomes the leader of the other. The absence of one of them therefore traumatizes the remaining one. It may take some time before the remaining Aby adjusts. The best way to comfort the remaining Aby is to always to give it as much attention as possible.

The situation can be very complicated to handle in case you have children. This is because Abyssinian cats get along very well with children because of their playful nature. Your dead Aby will not have just been your kids' companion but a valuable playmate. They are bound to take its death very hard. The best you can do in such a situation is to make your kids understand what death is and why their playmate has died.

Making sure your kids understand what death is and that it applies to human beings can be very beneficial to them. This is because kids learn through experiences and knowing about death will make them appreciate the fact that death is natural and can happen to any family member at any time.

## How to Cope With Your Aby's Death

Death of your Aby can be similar to the death of your child or a young family member. Knowing that you adopted or bought it, nurtured it to maturity and was a valuable companion that is no more can take a toll on your mind. Not only will you develop feelings of loss but also grief for your Aby. You will probably go into state of denial, develop anger and mourn before accepting that your Aby is no more. This may be the appropriate time to share your feelings with other family members. Doing so will no doubt go a long way in overcoming anger and feelings of loss that you may develop.

One reason why many cat owners choose to dispose of the bodies of their cats is to have the opportunity to remember their cats, knowing that they are buried in the backyard. Remembrance provides you and your family with a good opportunity reflect back on the good times you had with your dead Aby.

## Replacing Your Dead Aby

Having lived with an Aby that is no more will most likely drive you to adopt or buy another to replace the dead one. When to have another one will depend on several factors. One of the most important factors that may make it necessary to have another Aby soon after the death of the previous one is if you had two Abyssinians.

The loneliness that the remaining one will feel may make it necessary to get another one for company. You may also need to have another one soon after in case you have children. The other reason why you may need to replace your dead Aby soon relates to why you bought or adopted the dead Aby in the first place. You may simply like pets and Abyssinians in particular. You may also be used to having a pet as a companion and cannot do without one.

# Chapter 15 - Becoming an Abyssinian Breeder

## Who Is A Breeder?

With its beautiful short fur, clear eyes, perfect disposition and high intelligence, you may choose to become an Abyssinian cat breeder. The Abyssinian is indeed a very popular breed in the world and becoming a breeder of the same can assure you of a ready market, depending on your location.

Becoming an Abyssinian cat breeder means practicing the vocations of mating Abyssinians that have been carefully selected with the aim of reproducing other Abyssinian cats with the same qualities and characteristics unique to the breed. You can become a breeder purely for fun, as a hobby or as a business. Whether you choose to breed Abyssinians as a hobby or as a business, you will have a good opportunity to participate in professional cat shows and competitions. Becoming an Abyssinian cat breeder does not require that you must have attained a specific level of education. You must demonstrate that you have compassion and a genuine interest in the cat Abyssinian.

## Things to Note

Although you may have compassion and interest in the Abyssinian to a point where you want to become a breeder of the same, there are important things to consider. From the onset, becoming an Abyssinian cat breeder will not make you rich overnight. Becoming a breeder can be very expensive and you should not expect to recoup your expenses in a short period. You need to start breeding as a hobby before you can expect to start receiving some income. Indeed, most current successful Abyssinian breeders started breeding as a hobby before graduating to full time commercial breeders.

The second thing to note is that the practice of breeding requires commitment, devotion and time. Time in particular is very important. It becomes very necessary that you devote most of your time to your cattery. This is because the cattery requires daily cleaning, feeding, grooming and treatment of your cats. This is the only way you will be able to breed healthy Abyssinians that will encourage many in your neighborhood to buy.

Third, becoming an Abyssinian cat breeder requires some level of financial investment. You will need to construct a cattery at a suitable location, install the necessary infrastructure, buy cat food and engage the service of a vet among other costs. You will also need to incur other expenses in having your cats registered by relevant agencies and pay some fee to your local authority. Most current Abyssinian cat breeders stated off with only two cats in small rooms right within their homes, something that you too may consider.

Lastly, you need to be prepared to handle the emotional toll that comes along with the practice of breeding. The fact that you will be taking care of many cats and mating them means that they will be giving birth. It is common for some pregnant cats to die when giving birth in catteries. Others will die of natural causes including diseases. Kittens will also be at risk of dying of natural causes. Watching your lovely Abyssinians die will take a serious toll on your mind.

## Where to Start

The best way to start as a breeder is to prepare a room in your homestead to serve as your cattery on a temporary basis. This is not only cost effective; it will also be easy to manage your cats. Such preparation involves equipping the room with all the necessary equipment and supplies your cats will need to survive. These include food, water/food dishes, scratch post, bed and beddings and cat play toys among other equipment and supplies. You also need to engage the service of a veterinarian who will be responsible for treating your cats whenever they fall sick, become injured and in giving vaccinations.

The second step to becoming an Abyssinian cat breeder is identifying an established breeder from whom you can buy your Abyssinian cats. It is mandatory that you buy from an established and registered breeder. This is because such a breeder will be breeding pedigree Abyssinians that are properly registered.

You have the option of buying female-only Abyssinian cats in which case you will be obligated to buy a male afterwards. You also have the option of buying two Abyssinians, a male and a female. Depending on your preference and level of preparedness in becoming an Abyssinian cat breeder, you may choose to buy kittens or adult cats.

The fourth step in becoming a breeder is to register as a breeder. You have several options on how to register, depending on your location and preference. There are both national and international cat registries from which you can choose. International cat registries include UK's Cat Fanciers Association (CFA), France's Federation Internationale Feline (FIFe), UAE's Emirates Feline Federation (EFF), The American Cat Fanciers Association (ACFA) and The International Cat Association (TICA). National cat registries include UK's Governing Council of the Cat Fancy (GCCF), UK's Felis Britannica (member of FIFe), PRC's Cat Aficionado Association (CAA) and the Canadian Cat Association (CCA) among other national registries.

Registering your cats provides for several benefits. First, you will be recognized as a registered breeder licensed to breed Abyssinians. Secondly, you will have the opportunity to participate in both national and international cat shows and have your cats participate in different championships depending on their age. Participation in such championships can earn you good money depending on how your cats perform.

Thirdly, you will have the opportunity to learn better breeding techniques from both a registry and other Abyssinian breeders. Registering as a breeder also gives you the opportunity to know the exact breed standards you will have to maintain as an Abyssinian breeder. Lastly, you will have the opportunity to be appointed as an Abyssinian cat-show judge after gaining reasonable breeding experience. Note that you can register with more than one registry if you so wish so long as you are financially capable to meet all registration cost.

Different cat registries do organize different Abyssinian cat shows and competitions. CFA for example organizes the Kitten Shows and Championships (for pedigreed kittens aged between four and eight months), Championships (for unaltered cats aged eight months), Premiership (for altered cats aged eight months), Veteran (for both altered and unaltered cats aged seven years) and Household (for non-pedigreed cats aged four months).

Successful registration as an Abyssinian cat breeder is just the first step to becoming a professional breeder. Because the cats you buy will have been registered by their breeder, you will need to register all of the new kittens. This you will do with your original registry. Registering your kitten entitles you to a unique prefix that will be used as the first name for all kittens you will breed. It will be your responsibility to indicate a prefix you will wish to use.

Different cat registries have different requirements when registering prefixes. The GCCF for example requires that you must have been registered as a breeder for at least one year before you can register your kittens.

## General Breeding Information

Unlike other cat breeds, the Abyssinian does not become sexually active at a young age. Both your male and female Abyss will only be able to be sexually active with the female when it is between 10 and 15 months old. You will be able to know when your female Aby is in heat. It will become too vocal and roll around on the floor as if presenting itself to a male.

Your female Aby's gestation period is between 60 and 65 days. The last week of pregnancy will see your female Aby look for the most appropriate place to give birth. It will look for dark yet safe place where to give forth its kittens. Abyssinians generally give birth to small litters. Your female Aby will most likely give birth to three or four kittens, with most being males.

## Building a Cattery

It is only appropriate that you build a cattery once you have established yourself as an Abyssinian cat breeder. A cattery is where you house your cats for commercial purposes. Although yours will be a breeding cattery, you will also have the option of using it as a boarding cattery in which case other cat owners not able to travel with their cats will bring their cats to you for safe keeping at a fee.

It is mandatory that you apply for a license from your local authority before you can build a cattery. You also need to follow building guidelines provided by a registry. Every registry has minimum cattery construction requirements that you must stick to before you can receive another license from the registrar. A registrar will only grant you a cattery license after inspecting your cattery and certifying it to have met the set minimum construction requirements. Most registrars engage the service of local veterinarians to undertake such inspections. It will be the responsibility of the appointed vet to inspect your cattery on a regular basis to ensure that you stick to set breeding guidelines.

There are several minimum requirements when it comes to constructing a cattery, one of which is space. You cattery needs to be spacious enough to accommodate all your cats comfortably. The minimum space per cat is set at 30 cubic feet. In addition, you need to create a space for play, grooming and maintenance. Established breeders do go the extra mile to group according to their age, groups that are housed in separated cages as one way of preventing diseases.

The other very important minimum requirement you need to meet is to construct your cattery in such a way that it allows free flow of fresh air for your cats' good health. Your cattery should not only have enough windows but large enough windows that allow free flow, or air in and out of the cattery. Although Abyssinians are indoor pets, they need sufficient amount of light. You are therefore obligated to ensure that your cattery windows are not only large enough to allow free flow of fresh air but also large enough to allow enough light into the cattery. Artificial lighting may be necessary to achieve this if the windows do not provide for sufficient light.

Cat registrars are very strict when it comes to cattery sanitation. Not only are you required to construct your cattery in a clean environment; you will also need to ensure that there is a high standard of cleanliness in and around your cattery on a daily basis. Sanitation is one of the most important things that an appointed veterinarian will pay attention to whenever he pays a visit.

Such guidelines are not only requirements, they are mandatory taking into account the fact that failure to observe the same can lead to occurrence of cat diseases that can wipe out your cat population. Apart from such guidelines, you will need to have all the necessary supplies and equipment that your cats will need for good health and play activities. You will also need to engage the service of a veterinarian who will be available whenever the situation demands and when it is time for vaccinations.

# Chapter 16 - International & National Cat Organizations, Associations and Clubs

There are a good number of both international and national organizations, associations and clubs that are in the business of maintaining and promoting the welfare of cats, including Abyssinian cats. Most of the international and national organizations and associations are indeed cat registries. Cat clubs in particular are of special interest because they limit themselves to specific cat breeds, including the Abyssinian breed. Below are just a few of the notable organizations, associations and clubs.

## The American Cat Fanciers Association (ACFA)

Founded in 1955, ACFA serves the interest of cat breeders, cat owners, exhibitors and the general public in different ways. The association largely engages in promoting welfare, providing education, knowledge and enhancing interest in domesticated cats, both purebred and non-purebred.

Membership to ACFA is open to all including members of the public with interest in cats. Members receive several benefits including a copy of the association's regularly published ACFA bulletin that is published seven times in a year. Members also have access to many cat articles on the association's website, articles written by professional breeders and vets.

Membership to ACFA also entitles one to vote in the association's yearly elections. Members have the obligation to elect from among themselves who is to represent them in the association's board of directors. ACFA is also a cat registry that you can register your kittens with at a massive discount.

ACFA organizes cat shows at different locations in the USA, an activity that gives cat owners, including Abyssinian cat owners, an opportunity to show-case their pets and possibly win show awards.

## The Cat Fanciers' Association (CFA)

Founded in 1906 in the USA, CFA is the world's largest cat registry of pedigree cats. Headquartered in Ohio, the association has a mission to preserve and promote pedigree breeds of cats with the aim of enhancing their well-being. The current CFA cat breed registration stands at 43, including the Abyssinian breed. CFA has witnessed unprecedented growth since 2006 after its centennial celebrations, growth that now sees the association recognize 39 breeds for its Championship Class.

In addition to registering cat breeds, CFA also offers several other services to purebred cat owners, catteries and the general public. It has registered cat pedigrees that date three generations back.

Perhaps one of the most memorable moments for CFA was in 1994 when it hosted the CFA International Cat Show, the largest cat show in the USA. In addition to organizing cat shows, CFA is also engaged in setting and enforcing cat breed standards through cattery inspections, training cat show judges, supporting and publicizing research on cat issues, influencing cat legislation agendas and running cat breed rescue programs.

## Cat Owners Association of Western Australia (COAWA)

Founded in 1992 in Western Australia, COAWA exists as a cat registry and an advisory body to the Coordinating Cat Council of Australia. COAWA registers pedigree cats and provides a platform where cat breeders, cat owners and members of the public meet. It also registers non-pedigree cats.

In addition to cat breed registration, COAWA also organizes cat
shows including kitten, adult and championship shows. The
association currently has four cat clubs affiliated with it and
boasts a good number of cat breed judges.

## The Governing Council of the Cat Fancy (GCCF)

Founded in 1910, GCCF is the largest cat registry in the UK. It
largely registers pedigree cats. GCCF was founded by smaller cat
registries and is now an independent council with over 150
member clubs including Abyssinian cat clubs across the UK. In
addition to being a cat registry, GCCF also licenses cat shows
organized by all cat clubs affiliated with it. It currently licenses
over 100 cat shows every year. Apart from licensing cat shows
organized by its clubs, GCCF also organizes its own cat show
dubbed the Supreme Cat Show, which is usually the largest cat
show in the world.

## The International Cat Association (TICA)

TICA is the world's largest single cat association. Its membership
is comprised of catteries, cat owners and people interested in cats.
Based in the USA, TICA draws its membership from across the
globe including Africa, Latin America, North America, Europe
and Asia. It is a cat genetic registry that also registers new cat
breeds. In addition to registering pedigree cat breeds, TICA also
registers non-pedigree household cats that enjoy the same status
as pedigree cats in terms of cat shows and awards.

In an effort to enhance cat breeding, TICA has an elaborate Junior
Exhibition specially tailored for children who love cats, giving
them a good opportunity to graduate to senior levels as cat
breeders.

TICA has clear responsibilities that include registration of both
pedigree and non-pedigree kittens, formulation of regulations for
management of cat associations, licensing of cat shows organized
by its members, establishing cat breed standards, dissemination of

cat breed information, organization of cat exhibitions and education of cat owners, among other responsibilities.

## World Pet Association (WPA)

WPA is a body that exists to bring pet food manufacturers and pet owners together. It allows the two parties to interact through education and sharing of information. Most of its members happen to be cat food manufacturers, cat breeders and cat organizations and associations. WPA is the cat industry's premier trade association. It plays a very important role in disseminating information, educating and supporting research related to cat food.

## World Cat Congress (WCC)

WCC is a confederation of the largest international and national cat organizations and associations. It exists to promote understanding and cooperation among all the organizations and associations on matters that concern them. It encourages international cooperation among its membership on such matters as veterinary issues, legislations, pedigree issues and other related matters. Its membership includes FIFE, CFA, TICA, WCF, ACF, GCCF and NZCF among many other international and national organizations/associations.

Joining any of these organizations/associations provides for several benefits particularly if you wish to be an Abyssinian cat breeder. Such benefits include breed information, breed standards and general breeding information.

# Conclusion

Cats are not only lovely creatures but also very adorable. The Abyssinian cat breed in particular is very suitable as a pet. You will never feel bored when living with an Abyssinian. It is a playful cat that engages you all the time. It will always want you to give it attention, which is perfectly normal since it may be the only trusted companion you can have at home.

The Abyssinian is one cat that does not discriminate when it comes to family members. It is particularly very good with children with whom it develops a very strong bond because of its playful nature. Furthermore, the Abyssinian is very receptive to training.

According to research studies published in the Journal of Vascular and Interventional Neurology, living with a cat provides for several health benefits. One of the main benefits is that living with a cat reduces the risk of suffering from cardiovascular diseases including heart attack. Other health benefits associated with living with a cat include reduced risk of high stress level, reduced cholesterol level and reduced risk of depression.

Children raised in an environment where there is a cat grow up healthier. Unlike most cat breeds, the Abyssinian breed is very cost effective. It is generally a healthy breed that is less susceptible to common diseases to which other cat breeds are highly susceptible. The fact that the breed's kittens do not inherit serious diseases/health conditions translates into reduced veterinary expenses.

The popularity of the Abyssinian across the globe is not in doubt. It is one of the top cat breeds that most homeowners prefer to have in their homes as indoor pets. Its popularity is also evident in the high number of Abyssinian cat breeders registered by different cat registries around the world. It is also not surprising that you are most likely to find an Abyssinian cat club or association in every region of the world.

You can choose to have two Abyssinians as indoor pets or join the big league as an Abyssinian cat breeder. While you will have a loyal, lovely, obedient and valuable companion if you choose to have them as pets, you are also most likely to excel as a breeder should you decide to go that route.

## *Published by IMB Publishing 2014*